Street-Smart Guide to Valuing Business Investments

A Practical Guide to Value for Business Owners, Entrepreneurs, Angel Investors, VC Investors, and Business Buyers

Gerald. W. Barney

ISBN-10: 0615806333
ISBN-13: 978-0615806334

DEDICATION

This book is dedicated to all my former clients who created many thousands of opportunities to analyze business values and to develop the principles set forth in this book.

CONTENTS

INTRODUCTION 1
ASSESSMENT AND MITIGATION OF RISK 7
    How is Risk Measured?...7
    Mitigation of Risk 7
    A Realistic Look at Recovering the Investment....................9
    Calculating the Strategic Value.......................................10
    Negotiating From Strength..12
    Mitigation of Risk in Startup Situations............................13
    Conventional Theories of Risk..13
STAGES OF COMPANY DEVELOPMENT 17
    The Seed Stage 17
    Difference Between a Business Plan and a Strategic Plan.....17
STAGES OF COMPANY DEVELOPMENT 18
    The Start-up Stage..18
    To IPO or not? That is the Question 18
    Moving on With the Second Stage....................................20
    The Second Stage 20
    The Third Stage 21
PRE-MONEY VALUATION...23
    Upround and downround...24
    Definition of 'Series A Financing'..................................25
POST MONEY VALUATION 26
    Example of Post Money Valuation 26
HEURISTICS AS AN ANALYTICAL TOOL......................28
    What is Heuristics?..30
    Source of Word "Heuristics 30
    Benefits of the Use of Heuristics.....................................31
    When Use of Heuristics is Applicable 32
    General Process for Heuristics Analysis 34
    Heuristics Analysis..34
    How Does Heuristical Analysis Work? 34
    Self-Cancelling Errors..36
    Rules of Thumb...36

WHAT IS A VALUATION? **41**

What is Value – Really..41

Valuation vs. Appraisal

....42

Valuation vs. Assessment?..43

Appraisal Standards..43

Uniform Standards of Professional Appraisal Practice 44

International Valuation Standards 45

NACVA Standards 45

AICPA Standards..45

Asset Value vs. Stock Value 48

Basic Data Points to Determine MVIC 49

Determining the Normalized Net Operating Cash Flow

(EBITDA)...49

Fair Compensation for Owner's Work.....................................50

Personal and Professional Goodwill 51

Personal vs. Enterprise Goodwill 51

Family Law Situations 52

Goodwill Valuation in the Courts..53

goodwill valuation in the courts 53

Goodwill in Business Sales Transactions 54

Intellectual Property 55

Reasonable Royalty 55

What if IP is Used Internally Only? 59

Determining Reasonable Royalty Rates 59

IP Litigation..60

Comparative Ratio Analysis...60

MVIC From Market Transactions..63

Pre-Tax vs. After Tax Revenue Streams 65

The General Income Approach 66

Determination of Appropriate Capitalization or Discount Rate

....67

MVIC by Excess Earnings Approach 70

MVIC by Income Approach Using Ibbotson's Data...............71

MVIC From Pratt's Public Company M&A Database 73

MVIC Using Guideline Public Company Comparisons 74

MVIC by Discounted Cash Flow Analysis 77

Internal Rate of Return (IRR)..78

MVIC By Replacement Cost Approach 79
Putting It All Together – Reconciliation of MVIC 79
Adjusting the Balance Sheet to Market Value 80
VALUATIONS AND APPRAISALS **84**
Types of Valuations 84
    Asset or Enterprise Valuations 84
    Early Stage Company Valuations 84
    Equity Valuations 85
    Discounts for Lack of Control and Marketability 85
    Valuation of Intangible Assets 90
    Employee Incentive Stock Options 94
CAPITAL SOURCES **96**
Private Equity 96
    Friends and Family 96
    Angel Investors 96
    Angel Investment profile 98
    Venture Capital 98
    Venture Capital Financing Stages 100
    Private Equity Funds 101
Other Capital Sources 101
    Leveraged Buy-out 101
    Personal 401k Equity Investment 104
    SBA Loans 107
    Private Buyers/Seller Financing 109
    ESOPS 110
THE STRATEGIC PLAN **112**
Elements of a Strategic Plan 112
Sub-elements of the Strategic Plan 115
Sample Risk Assessment Checklist 116
INDEX **120**
ABOUT THE AUTHOR **122**
ABOUT AMERICAN VALUEMETRICS **123**

ACKNOWLEDGMENTS

My absolute thanks and gratitude to my partners: Melisa Silverman, Joanna Coy, Jim Lisi and Hao Wu for their contributions, experience and professional skills – all of which were incorporated within this book.

INTRODUCTION

This book has been written with the needs of very specific readers in mind. Its intent is to show owners of non-publicly traded companies and both current and potential investors in these companies how to determine, for their own purposes, what the company is worth so that they can make better decisions. Further it is to assist professional advisors in law, finance, accounting, taxation and strategic planning into getting a good handle on applied valuation. It is NOT a book on professional valuation or appraisal.

It is also NOT a textbook for business appraisers. Much of what passes for "business appraisal" is relatively recent. Until the Appraisal Foundation, under the direction of Congress, created the Uniform Standards for Professional Appraisal Practice in 1989 (under the FIRREA legislation) there was no universally accepted standard for business valuation.

The following is a list of the currently accredited valuation organizations which offer accredited credentials to business appraisers:

- American Society of Appraisers (ASA), since 1981

- Institute of Business of Appraisers (IBA), now part of NACVA, since 1978

- American Institute of Certified Public Accountants (AICPA), since 1997, and finally

- National Association of Certified Valuators and Analysts (NACVA), since 1991, (now the largest organization of business appraisers and which holds the highest level of accreditation of the group.)

It should be noted that the oldest is approximately 35 years old, and the newest, and by far the largest, is only 22 years.

As these organizations developed training programs, the valuation process moved more and more from the practical – (mainly the investment and market oriented community of brokers), to the theoretical, and in my opinion more pedantic academic community. The result is that many so-called certified appraisers have had *virtually no* experience actually valuing business for markets. They are in effect like the old joke about the consultant who can tell you 99 ways to make love but who has never had a girlfriend.

The result has been fairly predictable. Business brokers, M & A specialists, and the private equity investors (who invest their own money) in general have moved to alternative methods of assessment leaving the highly theoretical Fair Market Value concept for the IRS, Department of Labor, public investment specialists (who invest other people's money) and other government agencies which often appear to ignore the basic principle of value.

Street-Smart Tip

"Everything is worth only what its purchaser will pay for it."

- Pubilius Syrus, First Century B.C.

The above concept is often lost on the appraisal community. Much of the current valuation community tends to take the position that something is worth what its purchaser *ought* to pay for it not what the markets are actually reflecting.

But you might say "that is what appraisals are for!" You would be only partially right. Value is driven by the markets, not by the valuators – though valuators do issue what are sometimes, self- fulfilling prophecies. Let's discuss that. A conventional appraisal is a valuation opinion normally of a specific value at a specific time pursuant to a set of assumptions and using a highly structured process. It is usually done by a "Certified" appraiser. Though everyone probably intuitively understands that there is no single value that is "correct" the single value opinion is used primarily for tax and litigation purposes wherein a range simply wouldn't be feasible. (Try filing a gift tax return with a range of values on a probability curve). Though appraisers can give ranges, when they do it is usually for investment purposes. Ranges are also useless in public companies, other than the bid and ask for a particular stock.

Technicians track and invest on the movement of publicly traded stock prices, which themselves are usually not a good indicator of value. Fundamental investors *do* look at intrinsic value of a stock based upon its fundamentals, and when this is below the market price it indicates a buy, and vice versa.

Street-Smart Tip

Price and value are two different things. Price is what is negotiated for a transaction based upon each party's perception of value.

"Now-a-days, people know the price of everything, and the value of nothing"

Oscar Wilde

Value in a business investment is nothing more than assessing and quantifying risk. The more risky a business appears the less valuable it is. Investors who are interested in finding favorable risk/reward situations, and who are investing their own money generally are more interested in an assessment of the situation than a valuation conclusion. The assessment provides the reasons **why** a company has value over a range of assumptions, where a valuation conclusion picks one probable value, mostly for convenience.

An appraisal opinion is in fact a prophecy of what a business is worth based on assumption of events that have not yet occurred. It is essentially a probability prediction. And that's exactly what the discount rate used to capitalize income to determine value is – a probability assessment.

A conventional appraisal report typically states clearly what the appraiser's opinion of value is, but shows only enough analysis to support that opinion. It does not deal with many other analysis tools and methods that can give insights into current and potential future value that is needed by owners and investors so that they may make intelligent decisions.

Most appraisals are prepared in conformance with a set of published standards which will be later discussed in detail. These standards are often highly structured and may give the impression that a value opinion is being "proven" when in fact it is not. The standards typically outline a procedural concept for valuation. In some cases, such as AICPA standards, it is actually a prescribed set of operations. In USPAP and NACVA standards it is merely a collection of general concepts. We will discuss standards of value at length later herein. So, in a nutshell, this book is about "street-smarts" as opposed to "academic pedanticism." (Pedantics is defined as:

"A narrow, often tiresome focus on or display of learning and especially its trivial aspects: a pedantic writing style; an academic insistence on precision; a bookish vocabulary; donnish refinement of speech; scholastic and excessively subtle reasoning."

Where appropriate in this book I will provide Street-Smart tips which hopefully will assist in arriving quickly at an assessment of value. They will be "non-pedantic."

In the formal USPAP compliant valuation reports provided for maximum tax defensibility by our firm, the basic analysis is often in excess of 150 pages, and the entire report which includes an appendix of source material used in the analysis, brings it to a total of about 400 pages. All this to determine and defend a value. It is done because under recent tax court policy, the appraiser may not get a chance to testify, and his report as submitted will be considered as the only evidence. This means that if a subject is not addressed in the report it cannot be introduced and argued later. (The trial judge may allow testimony if he/she wants it for his/her purposes). This means that both sides (the taxpayer and the Commissioner) must advance their total valuation argument in the valuation report.

Conversely, in my role as a business broker, I am able to estimate market value using a rather short analysis, but only after careful assessment of the strategic plan and the company's financial statements. What I look for is the comparative risk. This is not an academic exercise. It requires considerable experience, the ability to interpret what is really going on in a business enterprise, and knowledge of the markets.

My knowledge of the business is based upon both an investigation by me, and/or my staff, and my experience. In my approximately 40 years of experience as a business broker, strategic planner, or appraiser I have valued somewhere north of 10,000 businesses. That is an average of about 250 a year, and is approximately the rate of our current valuation practice. Being successful in the marketplace requires street-smarts, not academic pedanticism.

The formal appraisal normally uses "Fair Market Value" as a standard of value (a term developed by the IRS). As you will see later, it is a hypothetical term, and I can say that I probably have never seen such a transaction in the real world, or if I did I didn't recognize it. Other standards of value are Market Value (International Standards), Fair Value (both legal and/or Accounting Standards), Investment Value, Strategic Value, Liquidation Value, Orderly Liquidation Value, Forced Liquidation Value, Intrinsic Value and Fair Value. We will explore these later.

So what can you expect if you read this book? You should have a good feel of what to look for to enable you to quickly assess a business' operations, strengths, weaknesses, and market position; and to reduce this to a heuristic (we will discuss heuristics later) analysis that will provide you with a sense of value that you can use to make decisions.

ASSESSMENT AND MITIGATION OF RISK

How is Risk Measured?

For investment purposes, risk is measured by applying a discount rate proportionate to the risk. We will deal with how to determine appropriate discount rates next, but first we need to understand some of the nuances of the use of a discount rate.

First, the discount rate (which in theory can be converted to a capitalization rate by deducting the long-term growth rate – whatever that is) can be used to capitalize a projected income stream by dividing the annual benefit by the discount rate.

So let's assume we somehow decided the appropriate discount rate is 10%. Let's assume an annual income stream (Net Operating Cash Flow) of $100,000. So with a 10% risk, what is this worth?

$100,000/10% will give you the answer. Which is $1,000,000.

An easier way to look at this is to simply divide 1 by the discount rate. This is the reciprocal, or inverse, of the discount rate. So in this case 1/0.1=10. So if you multiplied the income stream of $100,000 by 10 you would get exactly the same result.

But what else does the discount rate or multiplier tell us? Well, if the income multiplier is 10, and the income stream is pre-tax, then it tells us that pre-tax it will take us 10 years to recover our investment.

Mitigation of Risk

So now that we know this, how can we reduce risk in this situation? Let's assume this is not a particularly marketable investment. So the only way we can eliminate investment risk is to get our initial investment back. The faster we can expect to do that, the better, as until we have received it all back some of it is still at risk.

This, in fact, leads to the theory of risk management in closely held business investments. The discount rate is divided into two factors. One is the so-called "risk free" rate. A good surrogate for that is the amount of interest banks will charge you for a fully collateralized loan. It is arguable, but then again, we are only going to use our own assumption anyway. Let's assume that we have to get a 5% annual return on our investment to approximate a risk-free rate. In the old days, we could invest that in the money market or CD's and get about that rate. In today's market, small businesses can borrow money at about 5% even though the Federal Reserve is charging zero to the banks on a risk-free rate and paying near zero on deposits.

The other is the Equity Risk Premium – or in reality the amortization rate. Let's look at how long we are willing to wait to recover our investment. This will depend on the type of investment. Historic data shows that small business investors are usually willing to wait 5 years to recover investments in equipment. So this implies a discount rate of 20%. (Recovery in 5 years). But wait, the investor will want to receive a return on investment as well – in this case we have used 5%. So now we have to add the two rates to get to the total acceptable discount rate on an equipment investment (based upon the operating cash flow generated by the equipment.). The total is now 25%, indicating that the investor will receive 5% a year, and recover the investment in five years.

We have stated before that the appropriate capitalization rate is the same as the discount rate minus the long term growth rate. As the risk rate (capitalization rate) is reduced proportionate to the amount of expected growth, the effect is to increase the value.

If an investment is looked at that has a zero expected growth rate, then the capitalization rate and discount rate would be the same.

As a practical matter, during many years as a business broker, I have found very few investors who have done this kind of analysis. But they *were* aware of income multipliers. In the above example the 25% discount rate represents a 4X multiplier (1/.25) which is merely the reciprocal or inverse of the discount rate.

The remaining problem to be solved is to determine just what income stream we want to capitalize to determine the MVIC. This will be discussed in each section covering specific valuation types and approaches.

A Realistic Look at Recovering the Investment

For an established business, the previous section showed that the only way to eliminate financial risk in a non-liquid business investment is to recover the original capital. The "amortization" component of the discount rate is supposed to provide for that. But it is normally calculated on a pre-tax cash flow, so the *real* period of recovery will be longer than that. How much longer depends on the effective tax rate of the investor.

So breaking the discount rate into two components is a start, but it does not do everything an investor needs to know.

First, let's talk about effective tax rates. Accountants typically use the highest marginal rate to provide an allowance for payment of taxes. But a study of research by Professor John Graham as revealed in the 2013 Ibbotson's SBBI shows that 56% of the 3500 firms studied paid less than 10% in combined state and federal taxes. A calculation of the weighted average for all companies showed about 15%.

Therefore for investor, an additional component can be added to the discount rate for purposes of calculating how long it will take to recover after tax. The investor can either use his own effective tax rate, or perhaps the weighted average of 15%, to approximate the actual period of return of investment.

Here is an example.

- EBITDA is $1,000,000

- Long term grown rate is 2%

- Effective Discount Rate – determined from valuation analysis – 20%.

Aggregate capitalization rate is then: 20%-2%, or 18%. (Capitalization Rate is Discount Rate minus the LT Growth Rate)

The reciprocal of 18% is 5.55 which is the EBITDA multiplier. It also tells you that it will take 5.55 years to recover the investment with the above assumptions. The value would be $5.5 million.

Now, if the effective tax rate is 15%, the cap rate is now 33%, and the effective value to you, the investor is $3.0 million based upon your after-tax assumptions. Obviously the company is not *really* worth $2.5 million less. So how do you use this information? Easy. The value is $ 5.5 million. And your EBITDA is 15% less (85% of $1,000,000) which equals $850,000. Therefore to recover the investment in after-tax dollars will take $5.5 million investment divided by $850,000 a year, or 6.47 years. This signifies that it will take you an additional .97 years (let's call it one year) to recover the investment after tax.

Calculating the Strategic Value

Valuations determine what the value *ought* to be to an "average" investor (whatever that is). This is where the definitions of Fair Value and Fair Market Value come from.

But you, as a potential investor really need to determine what it would be worth to you given your situation. In many cases you can combine operations for a savings. You may have a better view of growth producing initiatives than the current management. You may gain some synergy in other ways.

So what you need to do is quantify that by starting with the income statements, or projected pro forma statements, both provided by the seller, or in an appraisal report, and modify them to reflect the changes in cash flow you believe you can realize. If it is based upon a discounted cash flow, you may believe you warrant a lower discount rate for less risk.

In short, you will prepare a pro forma, which will give you a different (hopefully higher) value for average EBITDA. Using the effective capitalization rate determined in the valuation report, you can now project a new value, which is the "strategic value" given your circumstances.

So continuing the analysis in the previous section, if the effective capitalization rate remains 18%, but the adjusted EBITDA using your own projections is increased to $1.3 million, then the value to you based upon these assumptions is $7.2 million. Therefore if you can acquire the company for $5.5 million it is obviously to your advantage to do so.

The Effect of Paying a Premium for a Good Company

It is often the case that in order to acquire a company that appears to be a really high-quality one will require paying a premium. Even if a company appears to be high-quality, if it has been run by a CEO for more than five years, and that CEO is also a principal owner, the chances are that there are ample opportunities for improvement. Especially if it is profitable.

Human nature being what it is, when a company hits a certain comfort level, and the principal owners are looking at the higher tax consequences of maximizing growth, vs. a comfortable life-style if they just let it hum along as is, they will often elect not to press on with what would appear to be obvious management initiatives and improvements. Also, if it is a company where the CEO is also effectively a COO, he may rather play golf than work.

These quirks of human nature can provide some significant investment opportunities. In some cases, the existing owners are reluctant to sell, and it will take a premium offer to make a deal. In other cases you may be in a bidding war and you need to decide how high to bid.

So if you elect to pay a premium what effect does that have on your recovery period? The math is very similar to the preceding example. But instead of estimating increased value by increasing EBITDA, you hold the EBITDA constant, and increase the value, which has the effect of lowering the discount rate. Using a continuation of the previous example, if EBITDA remains at $1,000,000 and you elect to pay a premium of $1-million (a total price of $6.5-million) then your effective EBITDA multiplier will be $6.5 million divided by $1,000,000, or 6.5. So it will take 6.5 years to recover the investment (pre-tax) in lieu of 5.5 years.

Negotiating From Strength

If you are a seller, you should anticipate the potential for a strategic value premium for a particular potential buyer, and also be aware of the slight increase in amortization (recovery) period it will take to pay you top-dollar for your company.

From the buyer side, if you pay a premium up to your calculation of strategic value, you really haven't actually paid a premium. If you offer more than that, you will have paid an actual premium, and you need to assess whether the increased period to recover the investment, both pre- and after-tax is warranted.

Street-Smart Tip

It is almost always better to pay a premium for a good company than to purchase a bad one at a discount.

Mitigation of Risk in Startup Situations

The percentage of ownership negotiated by the angel/VC investor(s) will be proportionate to the perceived value, which is ultimately dependent on the assessment of risk.

A likely feature of the financing agreement will be "clawback" provisions that come into play if milestones are not met.

The initial pre-money valuation will be based principally upon the founder entrepreneur's projections to which an appropriate discount rate is applied.

Each milestone that is not met may require issuance of more ownership interest to the angel/VC investor(s) which will have the effect of diluting the interest and value of the entrepreneur. This is also a good deterrent to over-optimistic projections of management.

There may be other protective or mitigative measures designed into the capital structure as well. The angel/VC investors may take their capital position in the form of preferred stock, notes or debentures which rank above common stock. These may have conversion features which could serve to dilute the entrepreneur's interest in certain cases.

Ultimately, if milestones are not met, the investors may have no further obligation to provide continued funding, and the venture will either fail, or the management must negotiate additional capital from other sources.

In the alternative, if at this stage, the angel/VC investors are not satisfied with the progress, and the cause is attributed to the management in charge, they will recommend or insist upon replacing all or part of the management team.

Conventional Theories of Risk

Investment textbooks generally show estimated risk by stages as shown in the following table. (Note – the risk rates equate to discount rates used to discount projected cash flows).

START- UP INVESTMENT RISK		
	MIN	MAX
Seed Stage	66.2%	72.0%
Start Up	53.0%	75.0%
Second Stage	33.7%	53.0%
Third Stage	20.1%	37.0%
Bridge/Pre IPO	20.9%	33.0%

Though this table shows interesting averages, how can one assess risk inherent in a specific venture without analyzing the venture? The answer is clear – one can't. So how does one determine a risk rate for a start-up situation?

My view is that a heuristic analysis of the elements of the business/strategic plan must be evaluated. I have developed model that allows a thoughtful estimate of comparative risk.

For a future projection, the key to risk lies in the completeness and defensibility of the strategic plan, or the business plan if it in seed stage. For a mature company it will be reflected both in the operating history and for growth in the strategic plan. We will discuss these in detail later in the book as they really are crucial to developing a defensible cash flow projection. But the summary shown below shows a way to start with the "static" discount rate found from market transaction (sales) comparisons of actual sales of operating companies, and the use of heuristics to "grade" each element of the strategic plan on a scale of 0-5, as well as to assess its relevance to the overall profitability and success. This will provide incremental increases in the overall perceived "risk rate" above the static rate.

We use a detailed score sheet for each item in the summary to arrive at our weightings. Though it is totally subjective, many tests of heuristics have shown that this approach usually yields superior speed and accuracy when used by an experienced analyst.

If all that is available is a business plan, with conceptual ideas only, the weights will be very low. If a fully developed strategic plan is available and shows not only what, but why and how the plan elements were constructed, the weights will be higher.

To put this in perspective, if someone came to you with a harebrained scheme, had only a sketchy business plan, no capital, and no real idea of what is required to reach profitability, you would probably weight every line item very low, and end up with a discount rate approaching 100%. If you apply that to his cash flow projections, it would indicate the project has a zero Present Value and is not worthy of investment.

If, on the other hand a person showed you a complete strategic plan, had industry experience, and the company was already producing and selling similar products in its current operation, you might only add, say, 5% to the basic "static" discount rate of , say 15%, and end up with a 20% discount rate – which for new ventures is really low.

	Cells in Red must be entered by analyst						
	Cells in Blue are automatically calculated						
Static Discount (from Market Comps analysis)	15%						
Static Value	85%						
	Importance Ranking (0-5)	Importance Weight	Relative Strength (0-5)	Relative Strength %	Discounted Value	Weighted Average Discounted Vale	Weighted Avg Discount
DISCOUNT RATE CALCULATION							
Mission Statement	2	6%	2.5	50%	43%	2.4%	
Market Analysis/Absorption Rate	2	6%	2.6	52%	44%	2.5%	
Absorption Rate Analysis	3	8%	2.5	50%	43%	3.5%	
Intellectual Property Threats/Opportunities	5	14%	3.5	70%	60%	8.3%	
Marketing Plan	3	8%	1.8	36%	31%	2.6%	
Pricing Analysis	5	14%	2.7	53%	45%	6.3%	
Competitor Analysis	3	8%	3.3	67%	57%	4.7%	
Operational Plan	3	8%	3.5	70%	60%	5.0%	
Staffing Analysis	3	8%	1.0	20%	17%	1.4%	
Operating Expense Analysis	4	11%	3.0	60%	51%	5.7%	
Cap Ex analysis	3	8%	2.5	50%	43%	3.5%	
Funding Sources & Uses	2	6%	3.7	73%	62%	3.5%	
TOTALS (WTD AVERAGES)	36	100%				46.9%	53%

The discounted cash flow for valuation purposes normally does not include calculations for capital needs. It is done to attempt to determine the value of MVIC, and it is assumed that the company has adequate capital.

The addressing of capital needs is not done in projections in the strategic plan. Nor does it deal with sources and uses of capital for similar reasons. The needs for these are all addressed with the discount rate which is a measure of risk. As the discount rate also contains an element of asset recovery, it in effect does effectively factor in real depreciation, and amortization as well as risk.

STAGES OF COMPANY DEVELOPMENT

The Seed Stage

The Seed Stage is the setup stage where a person or a venture approaches an angel investor or an investor in a VC firm for funding for their proposed venture. During this stage, the entrepreneur must convince the potential investor why the venture is worthy of investment. The investor will conduct an assessment of the technical and economic feasibility of the idea. This is normally expressed in a business plan. In some cases, there is a prototype that is not fully developed or tested. A business plan is normally not a fully developed strategic plan. It is conceptual in nature, and limited supporting analyses have been done to defend the projections – mainly because the strategic plan will cost more than the company has available before seed funding.

Difference Between a Business Plan and a Strategic Plan

The best way to explain this difference is by analogy. A Business Plan is a conceptual plan – analogous to "schematic drawings" for a real estate development. It shows the general concept, and develops a very rough hypothetical projection.

If the idea does not appear at least potentially feasible at this stage, the investor will likely not consider providing startup financing. However if the venture appears feasible enough to warrant an initial capital risk, the investor may invest some time and money in it for further investigation to develop the fundamental analyses and the preparation of a strategic plan. With a strategic plan it is possible to assess the potential risk/reward of the project. Prior to that it is just an idea. The provider of the first round of seed capital will likely require, as a condition of financing, provisions in the business plan for completing the strategic plan.

The strategic plan is analogous to "preliminary drawings" in a real estate development. These present what, why, where, when and how the venture will be developed. Each element of the strategic plan will be supported by specific detailed analyses. (See the section on strategic plans for details)

The strategic plan will also specify important milestones to be met and the additional capital requirements necessary after completion of each milestone.

At the seed stage, the risk of losing the investment is tremendously high. Most analysts rate risk at better than 70% which implies the compliment, or 30% chance of success.

Most analysts also are aware that the risks are less for angel financed startup companies, because of the conditions placed upon provision of capital requiring adequate strategic planning.

The Start-up Stage

If the business plan or preliminary strategic plan reveals that the venture is feasible the process will go to the second stage. This is usually termed the start-up stage.

At this point the entrepreneur really has two options. The best option is to secure financing commitments from the initial angel, or a group of angels, to take the venture further. Or, in some cases, the entrepreneur and initial angel may elect to present the venture to a VC firm.

The basis for this decision is whether or not the management intends to pursue an IPO, or whether it prefers to keep the operation private and gradually secure additional capital through private capital.

To IPO or not? That is the Question.

The principal advantage of an IPO is liquidity for the shareholders. Therefore IPO's are used typically for a "bailout" or liquidity event for founding shareholders, and not as a primary means of raising capital, though that is what the original intent of public offerings was.

The disadvantages are rife. Over the years the effect of the growing "nanny state" mentality in the United States, and the general anti-business bias of the congress since 2006, has resulted in much legislation, and worse, bureaucratic regulation which translates to:

- Higher costs of SEC compliance
- Disclosure requirements which are adverse to competitiveness
- Lack of nimbleness and flexibility
- Increased exposure to shareholder litigation
- Increased exposure to insider trading charges
- That unless the securities are qualified to be traded on a major exchange they are not very liquid in the aftermarket. And the exchanges have some pretty stiff requirements.

In the past several years I have discussed the efficacy of being a public company with a number of CEO's of small public companies, and to a person they would have preferred remaining private, and many were in the process of trying to take the company private through a leveraged buyout.

With the enormous increase in private equity investment firms, a large measure of liquidity still exists though certainly not to the degree of a public company. But then considering restricted stock provisions of the SEC this may be illusory.

The trend is pretty clear. In the United States, IPOs are in the wane in favor of various forms of private equity investment. Consequently VC firms are also in the wane – at least as far as their historic role in bringing companies to the point of an IPO. But management must make the decision as to whether the objective is an IPO, or to grow the company with private equity.

Moving on With the Second Stage

In either case a management team will be formed to run the venture. Either the angel(s) or a person from the VC firm(s) will take seats on the board of directors. Once a decision is made as to the capital structure route the company wants to go, the appropriate investors can be sought.

While the organization is being set up, if a product is involved, a prototype is usually developed and tested. In some cases, clients are being attracted for initial sales. Provisions are made for limited production.

To confirm that the assumptions of management are correct, the angel or VC firm will likely want to see an analysis of the strategic plan before committing to additional capital contributions.

The plan should contain the result of market research to see whether the market size is big enough, if there are enough consumers to buy their product. They also want to create a realistic forecast of the investment needed to push the venture into the next stage. The will also want to see an analysis of expected operating costs. A staffing plan and estimated costs will be needed to form a foundation for a well-supported cash flow projection. The projection should identify milestones that need to be reached to justify further capital investment. The cash flow projection should also contain a partial balance sheet which shows the projected remaining after-tax cash balance for each period – months or years. A five year plan is the norm. This is to insure that the "burn rate" does not exceed available capital during the startup period. A detailed list of elements of a typical strategic plan will be discussed in that section.

The Second Stage

At this stage, we presume that the idea has been transformed into a product or service and is being produced and sold. This is the first encounter with the rest of the market -- the competitors. The venture is trying to squeeze between the rest and it tries to get some market share from the competitors. This is one of the main goals at this stage. Another important point is the cost. The venture is trying to minimize its losses in order to reach the break-even.

The angel or VC firm monitors the management capability of the team. This consists of how the management team manages the development process of the product and how they react to competition.

If at this stage the management team has proven their capability, the VC firm will probably agree to provide financing for the next stage. However, if the management team lacks success in managing the company or does not succeed in competing with the competitors, the VC firm may suggest for restructuring of the management team and extend the stage by redoing the stage again. In the event the venture is performing badly, whether it is caused by the management team or from competition, the investors will likely refuse further funding.

The Third Stage

This stage is seen as the expansion/maturity phase of the previous stage. The venture tries to expand the market share they gained in the previous stage. This can be done by selling more of the product and having a good marketing campaign. Also, the venture will have to see whether it is possible to cut their production cost or restructure the internal process. This can become more visible by doing a SWOT or more sophisticated but similar analysis. It is used to figure out the strength, weakness, opportunity and the threats the venture is facing and how to deal with it.

Except that the venture is expanding, the venture also starts to investigate follow-up products and services. In some cases, the venture also investigates how to expand the life-cycle of the existing product/service.

At this stage the VC firm monitors the objectives already mentioned in the second stage and also the new objective mentioned at this stage. The VC firm will evaluate if the management team has made the expected reduction cost. They also want to know how the venture competes against the competitors. The new developed follow-up product will be evaluated to see if there is any potential.

The Bridge/Pre-public Stage

In general this stage is the last stage of the venture capital financing process. The main goal of this stage is to achieve an exit vehicle for the investors and for the venture to go public. At this stage the venture achieves a certain amount of the market share. This gives the venture some opportunities; for example:

- Merger with other companies
- Keeping away new competitors from approaching the market
- Elimination of competitors

Internally, the venture has to reposition the product and see where the product is positioned and if it is possible to attract new Market segmentation. This is also the phase to introduce the additional product/services to add customers.

As we mentioned, this is the final stage of the process. But sometimes there will be an additional continuation stage involved between the third stage and the Bridge/pre-public stage. However there are limited circumstances known where investors made a very successful initial market impact and might be able to move from the third stage directly to the exit stage. But most of the time the venture fails to achieve some of the important benchmarks the VC firms aimed and the process is modified.

PRE-MONEY VALUATION

A pre-money valuation is a term widely used in private equity or venture capital community, referring to the valuation of a company or asset prior to an investment or financing. If an investment adds cash to a company, the company will have different valuations before and after the investment. The pre-money valuation refers to the company's valuation before the investment.

Street-Smart Tip

The terms "pre-money" and "post-money" valuation refer to dilution calculations before and after ANY round of financing.

The term is somewhat misleading because it does not refer mainly to actual valuation of the company, but to the effects of dilution.

External investors, such as venture capitalists and angel investors will use an actual valuation to determine how much equity to demand in return for their cash injection to an entrepreneur and his or her startup company. This is calculated on a fully diluted basis and becomes the pre-money value.

Usually, a company receives several rounds of financing (conventionally named Round A, Round B, Round C, etc.) rather than a big lump sum in order to decrease the risk for investors and to motivate entrepreneurs. Pre- and post-money valuation concepts apply to each round.

Round A. Shareholders of Newco, Inc. own 100 shares, which is 100% of equity. If an investor makes a $10 million investment (Round A) into Newco, Inc. in return for 20 newly issued shares, the implied post-money valuation is:

$10 million times (120 / 20) = $60 million

This implies a pre-money valuation equal to the post-money valuation minus the amount of the investment. In this case, it is:

$60 million – $10 million = $50 million

The initial shareholders dilute their ownership to 100/120 = 83.33%.

Round B. Let's assume that the same Newco, Inc. gets the second round of financing, Round B. A new investor agrees to make a $20 million investment for 30 newly issued shares. If you follow the example above, it has 120 shares outstanding. Post-money valuation is:

$20 million times (150 / 30) = $100 million

The pre-money valuation is:

$100 million – $20 million = $80 million

The initial shareholders further dilute their ownership to 100/150 = 66.67%.

Upround and downround

Upround and downround are two terms associated with pre- and post-money valuations. If pre-money valuation of the upcoming round is higher than the post-money valuation of the last round, the investment is called an upround. If the reverse is the case, then the investment is called a downround. In the above example, Round B was an upround investment, for pre-money B ($80 million) was higher than was post-money A ($60 million).

A successful company usually has a series of uprounds until it is IPO-ed, sold, or merged. Downrounds are painful events for initial shareholders and founders, for they cause substantial ownership dilution and may damage the company's reputation. However, downrounds were common during the dot-com crash of 2000–2001.

Definition of 'Series A Financing'

The first round of financing undergone for a new business venture after seed capital. Generally, this is the first time that company ownership is offered to external investors. Series A financing may be provided in the form of preferred stock or convertible bonds or notes, and may offer anti-dilution provisions in the event that further financing through preferred or common stock occurs in the future.

Series A financing tends to occur when the company is generating some revenue from its business model, but rarely will the business be generating net profits at this point. Most series A investors will be venture capital funds or angel investors who are willing to accept the high levels of risk found in these early-stage company investments.

POST MONEY VALUATION

Example of Post Money Valuation

If a company is worth $100 million (pre-money) and an investor makes an investment of $25 million, the new, post-money valuation of the company will be $125 million. The investor will now own 20% of the company.

This basic example illustrates the general concept. However, in actual, real-life scenarios, the calculation of post-money valuation can be more complicated—because the capital structure of companies often includes convertible loans, warrants, and option-based management incentive programs. Further the appropriate multiple to determine to the enterprise value will likely increase due to decreased risk.

Basically, the calculation is the price paid per share multiplied by the total number of shares existing after the investment—i.e., it takes into account the number of shares arising from the conversion of loans, exercise of in-the-money warrants, and any in-the-money options. Thus it is important to confirm that the number is a fully diluted and fully converted post-money valuation.

In this scenario, the pre-money valuation should be calculated as the post-money valuation minus the total money coming into the company—not only from the purchase of shares, but also from the conversion of loans, the nominal interest, and the money paid to exercise in-the-money options and warrants.

As a more complicated example, consider a company with 1,000,000 shares, a convertible loan note for $1,000,000 converting at 75% of the next round price, warrants for 200,000 shares at $10 a share, and a granted employee incentive options of 200,000 shares at $4 per share. The company receives an offer to invest $8,000,000 at $8 per share.

The post-money valuation is equal to $8 times the number of shares existing after the transaction—in this case, 2,366,667 shares. This figure includes the original 1,000,000 shares, plus 1,000,000 shares from new investment, plus 166,667 shares from the loan conversion ($1,000,000 divided by 75% of the next investment round price of $8, or $1,000,000 / (.75 x 8)), plus 200,000 shares from in-the-money options. The fully converted, fully diluted post-money valuation in this example is $18,933,336.

The pre-money valuation would be $9,133,336—calculated by taking the post-money valuation of $18,933,336 and subtracting the $8,000,000 of new investment, as well as $1,000,000 for the loan conversion and $800,000 from the exercise of the rights under the employee option plan. Note that the warrants cannot be exercised because they are not in-the-money (i.e. their exercise price, $10 a share, is still higher than the new investment price of $8 a share).

HEURISTICS AS AN ANALYTICAL TOOL

We recommend the use of heuristics methodology as analytical tools for much of the valuation process. It is used in lieu of conventional statistical analysis where certain conditions exist as will be set forth below. Because it will be used in all the following analysis methods, it is important to explain it here.

Street-Smart Tip

Heuristics may appear to be complicated, but it is in fact "Street-smarts" in action. It is the way we make accurate decisions quickly, versus precise (but potentially inaccurate) decisions slowly.

The following abstract concisely sets forth one of many foundations for use of this methodology which has been extensively peer reviewed in a number of fields, including finance, psychology and engineering. The reference is an article in Psychological Review, Vol 103(4), Oct 1996, 650-669 By Gerd Gigerenzer and Daniel G. Goldstein, both well-known figures in the use of heuristics methodology. The abstract states the following:

"Humans and animals make inferences about the world under limited time and knowledge. In contrast, many models of rational inference treat the mind as a Laplacean Demon, equipped with unlimited time, knowledge, and computational might. Following H. Simon's notion of satisficing, the authors have proposed a family of algorithms based on a simple psychological mechanism: one-reason decision making.

These fast and frugal algorithms violate fundamental tenets of classical rationality: They neither look up nor integrate all information. By computer simulation, the authors held a competition between the satisficing "Take The Best" algorithm and various "rational" inference procedures (e.g., multiple regression). The Take The Best algorithm matched or outperformed all competitors in inferential speed and accuracy. This result is an existence proof that cognitive mechanisms capable of successful performance in the real world do not need to satisfy the classical norms of rational inference."

The Take-the Best Algorithm referred to is essentially the heuristic methodology we recommend for business valuation analysis as opposed to conventional statistical analysis because:

- The available databases do not represent the entire universe of businesses sold,

- Records are grouped by SIC, or other industry codes, which are arbitrary and which may include a number of entries that are not very relevant to the subject,

- The sample sizes available are usually quite small, often only a handful of transactions,

- The data is provided by limited numbers of cooperating brokers,

- The data is not directly verifiable,

- The motivations of the buyer and seller are not known,

- Total terms of the sale may not be evident,

- Data points usually involve widely varying gross sales, net cash flow and other parameters which affect value,

- Data points are taken at different times, typically within the past ten years,

- Definitions of cash flow may not be consistent (determination of "add-backs"),

- Selections are not random selections but are selected on the basis of apparent relevance,

- Price/Revenues and Price/Cash Flow curves are not normal distributions as required by statistical analysis procedures. They are generally skewed to the right indicating a much wider range of higher price earnings or price revenues multiples on the higher end, than on the lower end. This is because prices clustered at the lower end are, or are closer to "fixed asset liquidations", while on the higher end they reflect a wider variety of motives for purchase, such as growth potential, industry conditions, or general appeal generally referred to as Investment Value.

What is Heuristics?

Heuristics refers to techniques for problem solving, learning, and discovery based upon the innate human ability to recognize patterns. Where the exhaustive search is impractical, heuristic methods are used to speed up the process of finding a satisfactory solution. They are mental shortcuts to ease the cognitive load of making a decision. It is a predictive method (in valuation, predicting a value)

In more precise terms, heuristics are strategies using readily accessible, through sometimes loosely-related information to aid in problem solving in human beings and machines where there is not enough time, money or information available to analyze the situation using conventional statistical analysis methods.

Source of Word "Heuristics"

It is pronounced hyu-RIS-tiks from the Greek "heuriskein" meaning "to discover") This is the same source as the word "Eureka" meaning "I have found it." Human beings have an innate ability to operate in the world based upon pattern recognition. We induce "expected reality" from our recognition and analysis of patterns based upon our experience, and cognitive abilities.

An example of this would be the process of crossing a busy street. We see cars coming from both directions. From experience of the patterns we can judge about when the approaching cars will arrive at the crossing point, and make a decision as to when to step into the street to cross it.

An infant cannot make this decision because it does not have adequate cognitive experience to comprehend the significance of what it sees. The adult on the other hand heuristically analyzes the relative motion, comprehends the significance (consequences of being wrong ---splat!) and resolves it into a probability based decision to go or not go at a particular instant.

Pattern recognition is all-pervasive in our lives. Our ability to comprehend words, sentences, and the tone in which they are used, are all pattern recognition functions. We don't actually hear and analyze each word, or each letter; we recognize a pattern from which we can infer meaning.

This same pattern recognition coupled with our ability to make judgments about the significance of what we see and hear is essentially the process of heuristics.

Benefits of the Use of Heuristics

Heuristics evaluation falls within the category of usability engineering methods known as Discount Usability Engineering (Nielsen, 1989). The primary benefits of these methods are that they are:

- less expensive than other types of usability engineering methods and

- they require fewer resources (Nielsen, 1989). The beneficiaries are the stakeholders responsible for producing the product

It costs less money to perform a heuristic evaluation than other forms of usability evaluation, and this will reduce the cost of the project.

In the past twenty years, heuristics has been refined into a modern problem solving and analysis methodology, usually associated with systems science.

Heuristics deals with decision making where specific reliable data is not available, and the time and cost of obtaining such data necessary for a conventional statistical analysis is simply not feasible.

Heuristics is the art of drawing inferences when faced with limited, incomplete or fuzzy data. It is based upon the innate human ability to recognize patterns.

As an adjective, heuristic pertains to the process of gaining knowledge or some desired result by intelligent guesswork rather than by following a pre-established formula or mathematical analysis. For example, chess players use a heuristic approach.

As a noun, a heuristic is a specific rule-of-thumb or argument derived from experience. The application of heuristic knowledge to a problem is sometimes known as heuristics.

Other Definitions:

"Heuristics are procedures or principles that help their users work systematically toward a discovery, a decision, or a solution."
     -- van der Geest and Spyridakis (2000)

"A heuristic encapsulates knowledge and offers guidance."
     -- Farkas and Farkas (2004)

"A heuristic is a guideline or a principle. It is any observation that can be operationalized."

When Use of Heuristics is Applicable

Modern prediction methods generally involve one of the three following methodologies:

- Mathematical Analysis
- (linear regression, statistical methods)

- Heuristics

Both of the first two require highly organized and qualified data that meets specific requirements for analysis. Heuristics, on the other hand, allows analysis with

- Incomplete or fuzzy data
- Indeterminable sample size and/or population size
- More than one variable (multivariate data arrays)
- Non-Random samples
- When drawing inferences from similar but not identical data

As can be easily seen from the above list, all of the points are what are typically encountered in real-life problem solving. Therefore heuristics is optimally suited for business analysis.

Typical Uses in business analysis are for determining:

- Discounts for lack of control and marketability in non-publicly traded, exempt securities, where data is not available
- Value in IP or Patents, where there are multiple variables and data is not available
- Equipment appraisals where data is spotty, and quality varies
- Business Sale Comparison data, where there are multiple variables: i.e.:

  o Date (reflects economic conditions)
  o Motivation of buyer and seller are unknown
  o Divergent businesses in same SIC code
  o Deal points unknown.
  o Limited samples
  o Unknown population

General Process for Heuristics Analysis

- Define the goal or objective
- Identify the available data sources
- Collect possible data points
- If data is: (meets all criteria)
  - Abundant
  - Based upon a single variable
  - The population is known or can be estimated
  - Is a random sample

Then use Statistical Analysis, otherwise use heuristics.

Heuristics Analysis

- Look for patterns
- Look for limits
- Look for unrelated but indicative heuristics within limits
- Exclude those obviously outside the pattern
- Weight the data using the single decision algorithm
- Weight the sources relative to each other
- Use weighted averages

How Does Heuristical Analysis Work?

Humans use four judgment mechanisms in a typical analysis:

- Exclusion / Inclusion

- Limits
- Ranking of data
- Weighting of data or sources

Exclusion of Data. If data is encountered which does not appear to fit a pattern, it is best to exclude it.

For instance, if business transaction comparison data shows a 50x EBITDA price, and you are looking for the central tendency of P/E ratios for a subject which appear to be clustering around 5x EBITDA – exclude the data item. It means an outrageously high multiple was paid, or more probably that the sale was based principally on the value of the fixed assets and the company had relatively little net income. In short, a liquidation. In any case we usually cannot determine from the "comp" what the reasons are, only that it does not seem to fit the pattern.

Limits can be applied to data collection to eliminate cost and time necessary to evaluate all possibilities. For example, when looking for market comparisons for business sales, eliminating those with negative net cash flows reduces the number of possibilities.

Ranking: When hard data is not available, it is often possible for an observer to rank data based upon experience. For instance data can be ranked on an arbitrary scale of 0 to 5 as to the observer's opinion of relevance.

A ranking of zero can also be used to show data was looked at but disregarded as being non-relevant.

Weighting: Weightings can be applied either to data points or to data sources. Weightings can be applied based upon perceived relevance. This allows for refinement based upon experience.

Fuzzy Logic Process: Computers are good at arithmetic, they generally process serially and require discrete (binary) data. Computers are not good at generalizing, or dealing with conditions outside the prescribed domain possibilities.

Human brains are better at this, because they process in parallel and have extensive pattern recognition capabilities. This allows humans to process "fuzzy logic" and derive meaningful and useful conclusions from available data.

Self-Cancelling Errors

The effectiveness of using the heuristic methodology is greatly enhanced by dividing the problem into as many elements or issues as can be identified, and then rendering a weighting judgment on each of them, and ultimately combining them into a weighted average. Where particular elements may be over-weighted or under-weighted, there is a tendency for them to self-cancel. This process serves to quantify a whole array of judgments into a resultant value. As experiments done by Gigerenzer and Goldstein have shown, the results obtained are quicker, and more reliable than those done by conventional statistical analysis.

Rules of Thumb

No discussion of heuristics would be complete without a discussion of so-called "rules of thumb." A rule of thumb is a heuristic approach, and in some cases it can be helpful if used in conjunction with other heuristics to derive a conclusion of value. But used alone it may be very dangerous.

There are several publications available which promulgate formulas for valuation. These are mostly used by business brokers. Two principal ones are:

- Business Reference Guide, 9th Edition, edited by Thomas L. West, Business Brokerage Press, 1999

- Small Business Valuation Formulas and Rules of Thumb, third edition, by Glen Desmond published by

Valuation Press, Camden, ME, in 1993.

There are many other rules of thumb promulgated by industry groups.

The books are handbooks of formulas have been used to value businesses for years, principally by business brokers and small business owners. These rules typically fall into five categories:

- Multiple of revenues;

- Multiple of earnings (net income, owners discretionary cash flow, EBITDA, etc.)

- Multiple of book value;

- Multiple of a measured unit (Restaurant tables, hospital beds, subscribers, etc.)

- Formulas, like "5 months gross sales + inventory".

These rules should be treated as nothing more than a rough starting point. Unfortunately, these rules can lead to seriously flawed valuation estimates.

For business brokers, the rules are used mostly for small "main street" businesses, which often have, either intentionally or unintentionally poor accounting, and have no reliable projections of future performance.

The **multiple of revenues** is typically used in small businesses that use creative methods of accounting to reduce tax liabilities. In some cases cash is actually skimmed, which is illegal, and in other cases expenses are doctored to show less profit. This is common in small restaurants, for instance. But often an estimate of true gross sales can be made, and this can be a basis for a rule of thumb valuation. Dangerous, yes, but often the only approach. Valuation by such a method is not likely to be taken seriously, and business brokers often advise prospective buyers to engage in an observation period to determine for themselves what the actual gross sales are.

The **multiple** of book value is pretty worthless. Book value will not show the current intangible asset value – which is likely to be the largest of all the asset classes in a successful business. Also if depreciated book value is used, it may appear to have little or no assets. If undepreciated book value is used it may overstate the market value. In either case since the value of a business is based upon the *enterprise value* which is the total of fixed plus intangible assets, this approach simply is useless.

A **multiple of measured units** is likewise a very flawed approach because it does not deal at all with the profitability. And it is the profitability that creates value.

The **multiple of earnings** probably comes the closest to being useful. Its shortcoming is that it is based upon past performance, and does not normally look to the future.

The **formula** approach is often used in small cash-based businesses, usually retail. It has been widely used by a large group of buyers from "third world countries" who buy liquor stores, convenience stores, small gas stations, coin operated car washes, etc. It is largely a self-fulfilling prophecy in this community, and usually widely differs from what a conventional analysis would conclude.

None of the rules provide sufficient information to assess the uniqueness of the business, such as management depth, customer relationships, industry trends, reputation, location, competition, capital structure and other information unique to the business.

A proper valuation will go beyond formulas and include a full financial and operational analysis whenever possible."

Ironically, I have found that one of the most common mis-uses of rules of thumb is for valuation of accounting practices! A common rule of thumb for accounting practices is one to one and one half times annual gross revenues. This tells nothing of the profitability. If an accounting practice earns $1-million in gross revenues, and pays out all of it to sub-contractors or employees, it has no net earnings, and probably no real value. Yet the rule of thumb would value it at $1.0 to $1.5 million dollars.

The AICPA Consulting Services Practice Aid 93-3 Conducting a Valuation of a Closely Held Business, American Institute of Certified Public Accountants, New York, NY, 1993 cautions against exclusive use of these formulas, but goes on to state "…. *the valuer should not ignore what is being done in the industry. Frequently, an industry rule of thumb provides a representation of the perception that people have in the marketplace and should be one of the methods used in valuing the closely held business."*

The practice aid, while intended to be an educational and reference guide to be used by Institute members, did not establish standards or preferred practices.

The State of Florida, however, has put in the statutes that a business valuation performed by a CPA in Florida must conform to the AICPA Practice Aid 93-3"

Shannon Pratt, in his third edition of Valuing Small Businesses and Professional Practices, McGraw Hill, New York, NY, 1998, also cautions against exclusive use of these formulas. He does publish, however, the formulas commonly used for various types of professional practice valuations.

Rules of thumb are therefore of some interest, but are not definitive. So how should you use rules of thumb? The best answer to this is to use them as just one of several possible heuristics – *where they appear potentially applicable.*

- Reference to a particular rule might be included in the analysis, and then analyzed in context as to its reliability or credibility. But it can be important to show that the rule was considered, especially in valuations for tax purposes where the appraiser must show that he considered everything available.

- If valuation by the rule is not close to what is determined by more analytical approach, then point out the rule, and expand upon the reasons why it is not appropriate.

Street-Smart Tip

Rules of thumb are really only useful for businesses under $500,000 in annual gross revenues and/or where accounting records are not reliable.

They should NEVER be used alone, but should be included as one of many heuristics where appropriate.

WHAT IS A VALUATION?

Though it may seem like a silly question, it is quite basic to what we are concerned about. The following paragraphs should help make some sense of it.

What is Value – Really?

It is best to start with the basics. What creates any sense of value is human nature. That's why we see bubbles, like dot com and real estate. Humans like to think they make rational decisions. But in reality, they do not, and cannot. This may sound heretical to those that are trained in "rational business management" as is taught in most business schools. But if you think about it, a person never has enough time or enough information to make a truly rational decision, even if they could, and further to be totally rational one would have to know with certainty what the future would bring. Therefore decisions are *rationalized*, but not *rational*.

This is evidenced by markets everywhere. In a stock transaction one party is right, the other party is wrong. Both parties may believe they are rational, but in fact both parties merely rationalized their decision to buy or sell.

All of which brings us to the point. A valuation is merely an estimate of the probability of success (the compliment of the risk factor) applied to a general prophecy as to what the future will bring. It is not a fact. It cannot be proven. It is purely an opinion, and it is a *rationalized* opinion. And the opinion is based upon a set of assumptions, none of which may be actually valid. And worse yet, a valuation opinion is based upon the notion of a standard of value, such as fair market, fair value, or market value, which though it can be defined is not something really observable in nature, and is in reality a point on a probability curve which is difficult to define.

And though it purports to be stated as a value at the specified time, it is in fact totally dependent upon the prophecy of future events. However for tax and similar statutory valuation requirements it is necessary to state it as a specific value at a specific time even though it is merely a probability.

For investment analysis purposes, however, we must look at things differently. The valuation at a point in time tells very little of what we need to know to make a reasonable investment decision.

First, most investment decisions are made involving a company that has significant growth potential. Very few investors are interested in purchasing a dead horse. So the relevant issue is the potential risk vs. reward. This analysis is best done by expanding the "investment analysis" component of a conventional appraisal, as we will discuss further in detail. The investment analysis should give good insights into value for "pre-money" negotiations preparatory to bringing in early stage equity capital. "Post-money valuations are mainly pre-money valuations adjusted for dilution if any, and beneficial effects of the new capital in reducing risk, and therefore enhancing value.

Valuation vs. Appraisal?

What is the difference? This is a very common question. Technically, there is no difference in meaning and the terms can be used interchangeably. However, in earlier years "valuation" usually referred to valuation of intangible assets, and "appraisal" to valuation of tangible assets. Currently, based upon agreement of the major appraisal certifying organizations, their meaning is the same and they can be used interchangeably. They both mean the determination of the value of a defined asset, at a specific time, and under other specific assumptions, and following specific standards. They usually imply a specific standard of value and a specific premise of value – such as "continued operations," But the old definitions commonly are used.

Street-Smart Tip

Though the meanings of valuation and appraisal are technically the same, the investment community still generally uses the term "valuation" to apply to a business appraisal, and "appraisal" to apply to valuation of fixed assets, real estate, and discrete intangibles (Intellectual Property)

Valuation vs. Assessment?

If a valuation is the determination of the value of a defined asset, at a specific time, and under other specific assumptions, then what is an assessment? An assessment is the body of work used to determine *why* an asset has a particular value, from which the value determination is made. It is required in all valuations, but investors may want to take it further. It is the assessment that is crucial to most private investors.

The assessment is the process of developing a quantitative measure of risk. It is based upon a thorough analysis of whatever level of plan exists and consideration of current operating performance. Since a look forward is most relevant to investment situations an analyst will look to first the business plan, if it exists, and then the strategic plan if it exists, to assess risk factors and ultimately the appropriate discount rate. Business plans and strategic plans will be discussed in detail later. All valuations contain some form of assessment, but often additional analysis is done for investment purposes.

Appraisal Standards

There are two terms which look similar. One is "Appraisal Standards" and the other is Standards of Value. But they are quite different.

Appraisal Standards have been developed by various

appraiser certifying bodies and dictate:

1. How an analysis is to be done

2. How the report is to be prepared

For practical purposes there are four sets of appraisal standards:

1. *Uniform Standards of Professional Appraisal Practice* ("USPAP") are promulgated by the Appraisal Standards Board (ASB) of the Appraisal Foundation as amended January 1, 2008. The Uniform Standards of Professional Appraisal Practice (USPAP) are the generally accepted standards for professional appraisal practice in North America. USPAP contains standards for all types of appraisal services. Standards are included for Real Estate, Personal Property, Business and/or Intangible Assets, and Mass Appraisal. The purpose of USPAP is to promote and maintain a high level of public trust in appraisal practice by establishing requirements for appraisers. USPAP generally provides rules for Ethics, Competency, Scope of Work, and specific rules and standards for the Preparation and Reporting of appraisals.

   USPAP was developed by the Appraisal Standards Board of The Appraisal Foundation in response to the Financial Institution Reform, Recovery, and Enforcement Act of 1989 (FIRREA). Its standards have become mandatory for all federally related real property appraisals; it has been adopted by most states and federal agencies as a mandatory standard for all appraisal purposes. Because of this, it has become recognized as the "generally accepted standards of appraisal practice" and has been adopted by most appraisal societies and professional organizations as a mandatory requirement.

   The Pension Protection Act of 2006, and related regulations, set forth specific requirements for qualification of appraisers and appraisal reports in order to be acceptable by the Federal government (i.e. IRS, ERISA and DOL) which states specifically that....

"An appraisal will be treated as having been conducted in accordance with generally accepted appraisal standards within the meaning of §170(f)(11)(E)(I)(II) if, for example, the appraisal is consistent with the substance and principles of the Uniform Standards of Professional Appraisal Practice ("USPAP"), as developed by the Appraisal Standards Board of the Appraisal Foundation."

2. *International Valuation Standards*. These are promulgated by the International Valuation Standards Council (IVSC).

The IVSC is a not for profit organization incorporated in the USA, with its operational headquarters in London. The organization is mainly funded through membership subscriptions and sponsorship by valuation professional bodies, valuation providers and valuation users;

The IVSC is a membership organization and is open to a wide range of stakeholders including professional institutes, valuation providers, standard setters, regulators of valuation services and academia. Members are provided with a forum for participation in the work of the IVSC which can advise the Boards on agenda priorities. The IVSC currently has 74 member bodies from 54 countries.

3. *NACVA Standards*. These are promulgated by the National Association of Certified Valuators and Analysts. They are similar to USPAP standards and the two can be easily reconciled. However NACVA standards generally provide for more latitude in the appraisal process.

4. *AICPA Standards*. The American Institute of

Certified Public Accounts has issued the SSVA1 Statement on Standards for Valuation Services. It is a set of fairly rigid and prescriptive standards.

Standards of Value are the definitions of value subject to certain conditions. They are not specified by the various appraisal standards. They are dictated by the specific appraisal need and use. The specific definitions are:

Fair Market Value – The most probable price which a property should bring in a competitive and open market under all conditions requisite to a fair sale, the buyer and seller each acting prudently and knowledgeably, and assuming the price is not affected by undue stimulus. Implicit in this definition is the consummation of a sale as of a specified date and the passing of title from seller to buyer under conditions whereby: (1) buyer and seller are typically motivated; (2) both parties are well informed or well advised, and acting in what they consider their best interests; (3) a reasonable time is allowed for exposure in the open market; (4) payment is made in terms of cash in United States dollars or in terms of financial arrangements comparable thereto; and (5) the price represents the normal consideration for the property sold unaffected by special or creative financing or sales concessions granted by anyone associated with the sale.

Fair Value – Legal Application. A term that is sometimes used in conjunction with disposal of minority interests in a corporate or partnership dissolution through a repurchase of the interests by the business entity. It is essentially the pro rata Fair Market Value of the entire company without discounts for lack of control and/or lack of marketability applied. It is based upon the premise that the value of the minority interest is what would be obtained if the entire business was sold at liquidation

Fair Value -- Accounting Application. Though defined by hundreds of pages of interpretation, it is essentially the value that would be received by a company if an asset were sold.

Market Value. Defined under International Standards as:

The estimated amount for which a property should exchange on the date of valuation between a willing buyer and willing seller in an arm's length transaction after proper marketing wherein the parties had each acted knowledgeably, prudently and without compulsion.

Strategic Value and Investment Value are the value to a specific buyer based upon his own operational parameters.

Intrinsic Value-- is usually the value attributed to publicly traded stock when considering a 100% buyout by another party. It is similar to the equity value for a closely held corporation. It disregards any speculative premium that may exist in the publicly traded stock price, and relies on fundamental analysis and comparisons. It is most commonly applied to thinly traded (or non-traded) registered securities on the OTC bulletin board or pink sheets. It can be applied to any public company for M & A buyout purposes.

Liquidation Value -- Similar to a Fair Market Value except that it considers the seller not to be "typically" motivated, and that a lesser time-frame for conclusion may be imposed. In the business sale context, it usually refers to a value of the fixed assets only, but can also include the going-concern value if appropriate. It is a term most used by lenders to reflect the value of collateral for a loan. There are several levels of liquidation value; Orderly Liquidation in place (of the entire business entity), Orderly Liquidation of Components on a per each or less than total basis, and Forced Liquidation Value, which implies an auction.

<u>Premise of Value</u> – This is usually associated with the standard of value. It generally is an amplifying condition such as "continued operations" or "liquidation

Asset Value vs. Stock Value

This is an important and often overlooked question. Those who have worked in the markets for closely held businesses know that more than 95% of the time a sale will be an asset sale in lieu of a stock sale. This is because:

- In the case of sole proprietorships, LLC's and partnerships there is no stock.

- Buyers are generally reluctant to purchase the stock of a closely held business, especially if not audited, due to concerns over liabilities, both financial and legal, that they may not be aware of.

- The buyer will want to allocate purchase price so that he can depreciate and/or amortize the assets in the manner he chooses. If he purchases stock he inherits the assets at the depreciated value already shown on the balance sheet.

- The buyer may desire a different legal form such as an

48

LLC, partnership, or sole proprietorship. And if the selling company is a C-Corp the buyer may prefer an S-Corp and not want to incur any built in gain for an S-conversion.

Exceptions to this usually only occur if:

- There is a tax-loss carryforward

- There are contracts in the name of the corporation which cannot otherwise be transferred.

Basic Data Points to Determine MVIC

There are two basic data points from which MVIC (Enterprise Value) may be determined.

- Normalized Net Operating Cash Flow (generally referred to as EBITDA)

- Discount or Capitalization Rate – for use with the income approach.

Determining the Normalized Net Operating Cash Flow (EBITDA)

The following table shows a summary of the Income Statements. The calculation at the bottom adjusts the net operating income to derive net operating cash flow. Adjustments were made which will be explained in the next paragraph.

Adjustments were made to the following income statement to derive the two Net Operating Cash Flow measures (DCF and EBITDA) which are used as a fundamental datum to be capitalized to determine value. The two fundamental Cash Flows used differ only by the amount of fair market owner's compensation. Normal adjustments are to add back depreciation and amortization which are non-cash expenses;

and interest paid, which is a discretionary expense. In addition, other adjustments are made to "normalize" the cash flow. They include officer/shareholder perks, other discretionary expenses, and to adjust officer's compensation to fair market value. Weightings for each year were applied as shown above based upon the appraiser's opinion of relevance of that year's operations.

Add backs to the business included a Shareholder Perquisite for the owner's vehicle, Non-Recurring Expenses for litigation including legal costs, expert witness fees and customer reimbursements. There are also a Pension and Profit Sharing Plan and Officer's Life Insurance Premiums. And, there was funded depreciation for the replacement of capital equipment.

FY 2011 data received a weighting of four and was given the most consideration since it is based upon the most recent complete set of information. FY 2010 data received a weighting of three, FY 2009 data received a weighting of two and FY 2008 data received a weighting of one.

As part of the analysis, the appraiser would have reviewed the Company's financial projections for the next three years. Because the Company did not provide financial projections for the next three years, a Discounted Cash Flow analysis will not be performed. Because the economic environment is still unstable, it is difficult to predict with any reliability on future performance; thus, it was not necessary to take the projections into consideration.

The appraiser determined that the most recent four years income statements were adequate to discern internal trends and to establish a basis of value. Likewise, the most recent four years' balance sheets were adequate to determine internal trends but only the most recent balance sheet was deemed relevant.

Fair Compensation for Owner's Work

In the Analysis of Income Statements the actual compensation paid to key officers is adjusted out and replaced with estimated Fair Market compensation for the work performed.

FISCAL YEAR	FY 2008	FY 2009	FY 2010	FY 2011	2011 % Rev
INCOME STATEMENT ITEMS:					
Gross Revenues	15,442,244	14,877,073	17,207,449	20,254,832	100.0%
Cost Of Goods Sold	12,175,126	11,439,405	12,545,675	14,374,566	71.0%
Gross Profit	3,267,118	3,437,668	4,661,774	5,880,266	29.0%
Gross Margin %	21%	23%	27%	29%	0.0%
Expenses	2,336,453	1,868,568	2,205,582	2,380,165	11.8%
Other Income/Expense				0	0.0%
Net Operating Income	930,665	1,569,100	2,456,192	3,500,101	17.3%
Net Operating Profit %	6%	11%	14%	17%	0.0%
ADJUSTMENTS TO DETERMINE CASH FLOW:					
Officers' Compensation	333,147	367,953	502,038	542,038	2.7%
Other Shareholder Perquisites	9,522	9,522	9,522	9,522	0.0%
Interest	327	1,027	1,442	1,901	0.0%
Depreciation, Amortization & Section 179 Expen	770,760	766,059	811,424	926,177	4.6%
Discretionary Expenses				0	0.0%
Non-Recurring Expenses	187,737	1,440,957	13,533	26,912	0.1%
Pension, Profit Sharing Plan	181,850	82,093	89,383	92,701	0.5%
Officers' Life Insurance Premium	15,740	15,740	15,740	1,053	0.0%
Funded Depreciation - capital equipment replacement	-1,077,079	-433,231	-1,817,909	-1,245,624	-6.1%
Contingency for Uninsured Medical Costs					
Total Adjustments	422,004	2,250,120	-374,827	354,680	1.8%
Discretionary Cash Flow Before Officer's Comp	1,352,669	3,819,220	2,081,365	3,854,781	19.0%
FM Compensation for Officers' Work	333,147	367,953	502,038	542,038	2.7%
EBITDA	1,019,522	3,451,267	1,579,327	3,312,743	16.4%
WEIGHTED AVERAGES:					
Weightings:	1	2	3	4	
Gross Sales				17,783,807	87.8%
Discretionary Net Cash Flow (Before Owner's Comp)				3,065,433	15.1%
Earnings Before Interest, Taxes, Depreciation and Amortization (EBITDA)				2,591,101	12.8%

Personal and Professional Goodwill

Personal and professional goodwill is a subject that arises often in closely held businesses and professional practices. They arise in family law (divorce) situations, and in the case of business transfers.

Personal vs. Enterprise Goodwill

The non-discrete intangible asset value (goodwill) may be comprised of two components: enterprise/institutional goodwill and personal/professional goodwill (terms separated by a slash are essentially interchangeable). Goodwill which is created because of the persona/reputation/contacts of a key owner is termed personal or professional goodwill. (The terms are interchangeable and differ only in context as explained previously.)

Enterprise or Institutional Goodwill is the value that is owned by the company per se. Personal/Professional Goodwill is the enterprise value that would be lost if the key person at issue were to leave the enterprise, and worse, compete with it. It occurs frequently in small private companies. It is rarely a significant factor in larger companies. From a valuation point of view it is actually a liability of the company when considering the value of an enterprise.

In the real world, mitigation is usually achieved with a non-compete agreement, and an employment agreement (or continued minority interest) for a reasonable period of time after which it is presumed the clientele will have become comfortable with the new owner(s), developed a working relationship with the new owners, and not take their business elsewhere once a sale is completed.

Family Law Situations.

There are three issues that must be addressed in valuing business interests for the purposes of property settlements in family law. They are:

- Personal vs. institutional goodwill (personal and professional goodwill are similar in nature – personal applies to all types of companies and professional applies to professional practices (i.e. medical practice, law firm, etc.)

- Intellectual properties that may be held by a divorcing spouse, or by the business entity.

- Minority interests in business investments, which may dictate substantial discounts in value for lack of control and/or lack of marketability.

Goodwill Valuation in the Courts

How do the courts treat goodwill in family law matters? To understand this issue it is necessary to first put it in the perspective of the various laws in the 50 states plus the District of Columbia. The first issue with seeking guidance from the court cases is their date. Until the Appraisal Foundation, under the direction of Congress, created the Uniform Standards for Professional Appraisal Practice in 1989 (under the FIRREA legislation) there was no universally accepted standard for business valuation.

The "prevailing cases" in nine states occurred before USPAP was implemented and before the formation of the now existing system of appraiser qualification and accreditation. There were no standards. California has the most ancient prevailing case –In re Marriage of Foster, 42 Cal. App. 3d, 577, 1974.

The trends from the court cases show that as of 2011 there is still considerable disagreement amongst the states as regards goodwill in marital estates:

- 13 States hold that both institutional and professional goodwill are marital assets (This is true of California)

- 28 States hold that institutional but not professional goodwill is a marital asset

- 1 State has no decisions at all

- 5 States have no clear resolution

- 4 States hold that neither institutional nor professional goodwill is a marital asset

(Washington, DC is included as a state, hence a total of 51.)

Generally speaking, the 28 states holding that institutional goodwill is a marital asset and professional goodwill is not, have, except for one, prevailing cases dated after USPAP was implemented in 1989. This appears to be the most defensible position in light of modern valuation practice. Therefore, in the 13 states which reflect both as marital assets, there is an opportunity to argue the differences on the merits because of the new standards and better valuation methodologies and showing that the "prevailing case" is based upon antiquated information and procedures.

Goodwill in Business Sales Transactions

The issue of Personal/Professional goodwill is more than a theoretical problem for buyers or investors – and therefore for sellers. If a business has been successful based on the persona, skill, experience and contacts of one or more key officers or employees, a significant portion of value could be lost if these people do not stay on board.

The business owners should analyze the situation, and take whatever legal steps are available in their state to cement a non-compete agreement into an employment agreement. This is very complicated law, and business owners should pay for this expertise. Key people can hurt the business in two important ways. They can divulge proprietary information to an outside party – usually a competitor who is interested in hiring them, and/or they can take key relationships with customers and vendors with them. They can also "poison the air" with false rumors that can hurt the company.

Investors or buyers should carefully evaluate this potential. They are in position to make a sale subject to reaching a satisfactory employment agreement with these people. A far better solution than trying to chase the horse once he's gotten out of the barn.

In any case, when it comes to valuation of the business, if a business has exposure to this, and has not mitigated this exposure legally, with a non-compete agreement and/or a confidentiality agreement, and an employment agreement that is assignable to the buyer, then a competent valuator will impute a contingent liability for loss of this portion of goodwill in the adjusted balance sheet. This can seriously jeopardize both the transaction and potential financing.

Street-Smart Tip

Pay close attention to the possibility of the existence of personal/professional goodwill and deal with protecting it as effectively as possible before a problem exists. You will need legal advice

---

Intellectual Property

Intellectual Property is one of the discrete intangible assets. As such it can be sold separately from the sale of a business. If such property exists, it should be valued and placed on the adjusted balance sheet for valuation purposes. Though it is an intangible asset, it is not part of goodwill – or the non-discrete intangible assets.

Damages. The fair value of IP is often required for financial reporting. However, valuation in some form is also needed to determine a claim for damages. The following table shows the common claims for IP damages by type, and the theories of damages that apply:

Patent	Trademark	Copyright	Trade Secret
Lost Profits	Lost Profits	Lost Profits	Lost Profits
	Unjust Enrichment	Unjust Enrichment	Unjust Enrichment
Royalty	Royalty	Royalty	Royalty
	Corrective Advertising		Head Start

For Intellectual Property, the owner is entitled to a reasonable royalty. This is the most common basis for determining damages for infringement. Others may include lost profits and unjust enrichment. The reasonable royalty is the principal basis for determining value.

For IP that is licensed to others, and for which royalties are paid, valuation is generally based upon the capitalized value of the anticipated royalty income stream over the life of the IP. The valuation process can be quite complex, but the fundamentals to value remain the same.

Copyrights. Copyright protection provides protection for original works of authorship fixed in any tangible medium of expression from which they can be perceived, reproduced, or otherwise communicated, either directly or with the aid of a machine or device. Such works generally include:

> Literary works;
> Musical works;
> Dramatic works;
> Pantomimes and choreographic works;
> Pictorial, graphic and sculptural works;
> Motion pictures and other audio-visual works;
> Sound recordings; and
> Architectural works.

As a general rule, copyrights do not require registration with the U. S. Copyright Office. Copyright protection attaches immediately upon creation of the work. Moreover, the fair use doctrine permits limited copying and sampling. However damages are often more difficult to prove and collect, unless the copyright is registered. Copyright damages are established by Title 17, Section 504 of the U.S. Code. See 17 U.S.C. §504.

Lost Profits. In a lost profits case for damages from lost sales, *Panduit Corp v. Stahlin Bros. Fibre Works, Inc. 575 F.2d 1152, 1164 (6th Cir. 1978)*, determined that the standard test for lost profits requires that the four Panduit factors must be met:

1. There is demand for the product;
2. There are no acceptable non-infringing alternatives;
3. The company has the capacity to service the sales claimed; and
4. Lost profits damages are quantifiable.

Furthermore, the entire market rule must be addressed. The entire market rule permits recovery of damages based upon the fact that the non-patented product cannot be sold without the patented feature. *See State Industries, Inc. v. Mor-Flo Industries, Inc., F. 2d 1573 (1989) and Cornell University v. Hewlett-Packard Co., 609 F. Supp. 2d 279 (2009)*.

This rule is intended to limit the value of IP to the actual, proportionate, role it plays in the generation of profits. A patent on a minor component of a product does not entitle the owner rights to all the profits on the products, but only a reasonable royalty based upon its comparative contribution.

Royalties. The fifteen factors to be addressed in quantifying royalty related damages in a patent infringement case were addressed in the landmark case *Georgia Pacific Corp. v. U.S. Plywood Corp, 318 F Supp. 1116, 116 U.S.P.Q. 235 (SDNY 1970)*. The factors include:

1. The royalties received by the company for licensing the patent, proving or tending to prove an established royalty.

2. The rates paid by the licensee for the use of other similar patents.

3. The nature and scope of the license, such as whether it is exclusive or nonexclusive, restricted or non-restricted in terms of territory or customers.

4. The company's policy of maintaining its patent monopoly by licensing the use of the invention only under special conditions designed to preserve the monopoly.

5. The commercial relationship between the company and licensees, such as whether they are competitors in the same territory, in the same line of business or whether they are inventor and promoter.

6. The effect of selling the patented specialty in promoting sale of other company products; the existing value of the invention to the company as a generator of sales of nonpatented items; and the extent of such derivative or "convoyed" sales.

7. The duration of the patent and the term of the license.

8. The established profitability of the patented product, its commercial success and its current popularity.

9. The utility and advantages of the patent property over any old modes or devices that had been used.

10. The nature of the patented invention, its character in the commercial embodiment owned and produced by the licensor, and the benefits to those who used it.

11. The extent to which the infringer used the invention and any evidence probative of the value of that use.

12. The portion of the profit or selling price that is customary in the particular business or in comparable businesses.

13. The portion of the realizable profit that should be credited to the invention as distinguished from any

nonpatented elements, manufacturing process, business risks or significant features or improvements added by the infringer.

14. The opinion testimony of qualified experts.

15. The amount that the company and a licensee would have agreed upon at the time the infringement began if they had reasonably and voluntarily tried to reach an agreement.

A discussion of these factors is beyond the scope of this book, but in general they raise specific issues that should be addressed to derive an opinion as to the value of a royalty that should be due to an IP owner. While the opinion as to value is derived qualitatively, the factors provide the foundation for a heuristic analysis to determine a quantifiable result.

What if IP is Used Internally Only?

IP being created and used for internal purposes only is a very common situation. Under this circumstance, the company may not be able to determine which portion of its net income is attributable to internally generated and used IP. Nevertheless, the IP may still be valued by: 1) determining a reasonable royalty rate it would pay for use of the IP; 2) adjusting the cash flow downward to reflect this as an expense; and 3) capitalizing the anticipated royalties to determine the value of the IP. The value of the IP is then added to the balance sheet as a discrete intangible asset. For purposes of valuation, it is assumed that if the IP were sold, the company would obtain a license for use from the buyer as a condition of the sale. That said, this does not change the book value accounting used for tax purposes.

Determining Reasonable Royalty Rates

Reasonable royalty rates can be determined in multiple ways. There are several databases available which show rates paid for various types of IP. Access is relatively expensive. It is the appraiser's job to analyze them, and to attempt to derive the most defensible rate from this data. Often situations arise where a company has licensed its IP to another person/company at a rate either higher or lower than a "reasonable rate" for business reasons. Does this bind the company to that rate? No, it does not.

IP Litigation

IP disputes are commonplace – though very few (perhaps less than 3%) of cases actually go to trial, and most settle. But until settled they remain part of the litigation process and impair value.

Many of these cases are lost profits claims. In very few cases is diminution of value an issue. As this is essentially business litigation, once both sides are fully aware of the potential damages the vast majority of cases are settled or dropped. An infringer has the option of paying the royalty, plus costs, or reaching an alternative settlement such as a buyout. A defender may elect to settle rather than risk a loss, as infringement lost profits damages can be difficult to quantify defensibly.

The most salient and practical point is that both sides of an IP damages suit will find it highly advantageous to have a valuation assessment by a forensic financial analyst to fully appreciate the strengths and weaknesses of both side's position. If unable to settle, it prepares the parties for trial. In short, an intelligent settlement decision may be made if one knows and can judge the strength of each side's claims.

Comparative Ratio Analysis

The ratio analysis below shows how the company compares

with the industry averages provided by Integra, one of several industry data providers. This analysis, along with a detailed analysis of strengths and weaknesses prepared in conjunction with the Income Approach analysis provides a basis for adjusting the discount rate to reflect more or less risk, which in turn adds a premium or a discount to the resulting value.

COMPARATIVE RATIO ANALYSIS

	IDEAL SCENARIO	INDUSTRY	SUBJECT	COMPARISON CO to INDUSTRY
Revenue Grow th	Higher is better	0.050	0.177	Better Than Industry
Quick Ratio	Higher is better	1.42	1.90	Better Than Industry
Current Ratio	Higher is better	1.91	2.25	Better Than Industry
Accounts Receivable/Sales	Low er is better	0.14	0.14	Worse Than Industry
Total Debt to Assets	Low er is better	0.55	0.44	Better Than Industry
Pre-tax Return on Assets	Higher is better	0.05	0.25	Better Than Industry
Pre-tax Return on Net Worth	Higher is better	0.10	0.44	Better Than Industry
Working Capital to Sales	Higher is better	0.15	0.24	Better Than Industry
Operating Income (EBIT) to Sales	Higher is better	0.032	0.17	Better Than Industry

---

Street-Smart Tip

Comparative Ratio Analysis can only tell you whether the subject is performing better or worse than industry averages, and by how much. The fact is, the industry averages for any particular criteria may be totally irrelevant. It is linked to a specific industry code, which may not be totally appropriate for the subject, which may operate within several industry codes.

In an asset sale, the collection of assets being transferred is comprised of the enterprise value (fixed plus non-discrete intangible assets – well get into these later) plus real estate, if it exists, as a separate transaction. The buyer may also purchase the merchandise inventory if it exists, or a portion of it if he feels the company has excessive inventory. Receivables usually remain with the seller, though in some cases an arrangement is made to purchase those as well. Normally, liabilities remain with the seller, unless there is a negotiation to assume part or all of them in the transaction.

Therefore, the key assets comprising the enterprise value are valued separately. And again, they are comprised of fixed plus intangible assets in an asset sale.

One other asset class has not been discussed. It is Intellectual Property and/or other discrete intangible assets. These will be discussed in detail in a later section. Sometimes these are included in the enterprise value if the company only uses them internally. However if they are licensed to third parties they may be exempted from the sale, and licensed to the purchasing party.

In transaction databases available to appraisers the enterprise value is also commonly referred to as the Market Value of Invested Capital, and the acronym MVIC is used to signify this.

MVIC is important, because all of the methods of valuing a company first require determining the value of MVIC. In an asset sale the price will usually be spelled out in the purchase and sale agreement.

In an equity valuation for a stock sale, the MVIC must be integrated into an adjusted balance sheet. In this exercise the balance sheet is adjusted to market value at whatever standard is selected. The MVIC will be the total of fixed plus intangible assets. Intangible assets are found by deducting the appraised value of the fixed assets from MVIC.

The reason for combining fixed plus intangible assets to obtain the MVIC is that this is the value that can be determined from a variety of approaches as will be outlined in the next paragraphs.

When the total MVIC is found, the value of the fixed assets, which may be determined by estimate or by appraisal, can be subtracted to obtain the intangible asset value – e.g. goodwill.

Street-Smart Tip

In most cases it is not important that a fixed asset appraisal be done, and the depreciated book value can be used as a surrogate for fair market value.

If the value of fixed assets is over or under stated it will be automatically be offset by a corresponding change in intangible asset value so that the total MVIC remains the same.

In most cases the depreciated book value of fixed assets (does not include real estate) is very close to what the appraised fair value would be. This is not true where fixed assets either hold their value better than the rates used for tax purposes, or where they actually appreciate, which can happen with certain types of assets.

MVIC From Market Transactions

Fairly reliable inferences as to value come from market comparisons. In general these ratios tend to be quite stable over time, and comparisons with sales of similar businesses sold within the past ten years or so are equally valid The most reliable databases for small business comparative sales are the BizComps and Pratt's Stats Databases, and for larger small businesses, the Pratt's Public Company M & A transaction database. Inferences can be gleaned from them using a heuristics analysis methodology, where the comparisons are weighted by the appraiser's judgment as to relative reliability and similarity to the subject on a scale of 0 to 5. Such factors as date of transaction, price/earnings ratios, and gross sales, as well as the description of the business are considered to develop the subjective weighting. The values found are the total of fixed assets and non-discrete (goodwill) intangible assets (MVIC) and exclude discrete intangible assets such as Intellectual Property, which if it exists is treated separately on the balance sheet and must be appraised separately.

Street-Smart Tip

The comparative sales (market approach) does not take into account the strengths and weaknesses of the subject company. It should be used only to determine representative BASIC or "Static" discount rates for similar businesses. These must be adjusted for strengths and weaknesses using the income approach.

Street-Smart Tip

Though conventional appraisals use comparative sales data based upon SIC and similar codes, in fact the codes are rather arbitrary and can be misleading. There are a wide variety of business models found in every code. The most relevant comps are found in looking at similar business models, which generally exhibit similar profitability profiles and similar risk profiles. This is far more relevant than an arbitrary SIC code.

Pre-Tax vs. After-Tax Revenue Streams

People who have been active in the buying, selling or investing in closely held businesses know that better than 95% of businesses are sold as asset sales, not stock sales. We have gone through the reasons elsewhere. But it points up an important fact to consider. The principal asset being sold is the Enterprise Value, or MVIC. Anything else is basically cash or an equivalent. Virtually no business buyer cares what the existing structure is (C or S Corporation, LLC, partnership or sole proprietorship). They are interested in purchasing the enterprise system – which in systems terminology is the "transform" which converts investment to a profit stream. Further a buyer can usually elect whatever organizational form he wants. So valuation should always done on the pre-tax revenue stream.

The fact is that EBITDA is the most universal datum for value. EBITDA must also be normalized – that is-- unusual and non-operating income/expenses are adjusted out. But it is a pre-tax benefit stream.

The Seller's Discretionary Earnings, or Discretionary Cash Flow are also often used for very small businesses that file Schedule C's on their 1040 tax return. This datum is essentially EBITDA before fair compensation to the owner/operator for work he performs. The income shown on the Schedule C is not the net cash flow for the business, it is the self-employment income of the operator. It can be converted to EBITDA by deducting imputed fair compensation for the owner's work to normalize the statement.

But you might ask "what if you are valuing the stock of a corporation?" Shouldn't you use after-tax income? The answer is if you do it correctly, you value the enterprise value pre-tax, and adjust the balance sheet to show fixed and intangible assets at market value. If there are tax considerations that affect the balance sheet, they will still be there.

The General Income Approach

This approach requires the application of a risk premium
component of the discount rate or a capitalization rate. The
capitalization rate is normally applied to historic/current
earnings, and the discount rate is used for discounted cash
flows of future earnings. They are related. Theoretically, the
Capitalization rate equals the Discount Rate minus the Long
Term Growth Rate. The problem is that I have not yet met
anyone who could actually predict the long term growth rate.
Adding a factor for inflation is not the same as a long term
growth rate. It is really just adjusting the currency value from
nominal dollars into real (inflation adjusted) dollars.

Historic discount rates can be inferred directly from market
comparisons. Alternatively, there are tools available, such as
Duff and Phelps and Morningstar's Ibbotson's SBBI, from
which discount rates can be estimated using the "build up"
method based upon derivative data from public companies.
While these appear superficially to be precise quantitative
methods of determining appropriate discount rates because

they are based upon data from public companies, to develop an appropriate discount rate for a non-registered, non-publicly traded, closely held security requires a great deal of subjective input requiring experience in analyzing such enterprises. In the Ibbotson's approach risk factors such as "specific company risk" and "intangible earnings factor" must be added, as well as determining the long term sustainable growth rate. There are simply no data sources for such factors, and they must be applied by the appraiser on the basis of judgment and experience, and his own analysis.

The risk premium is in theory (and is evidenced by actual market comparisons) the additional return needed to mitigate financial risk, which translates to a recovery of the investment within an acceptable period of time in the face of the illiquidity of the non-publicly traded security.

Determination of Appropriate Capitalization or Discount Rate

The first step in a valuation by the Income Approach is to determine the appropriate capitalization or discount rate. Capitalization rates are used to capitalize current/historic EBITDA or SDE (Seller's Discretionary Earnings) to a Present Value. Discount rates are used to capitalize the value of a projected income or benefit stream to a Present Value.

There are two general approaches available to do this. One is to seek discount rate comparisons from actual market transactions. The other is to use a so-called "build up" process whereby basic risk rate components from publicly traded companies are used as a basis and then additional factors for industry risk, company specific risk, size, and beta are applied. (Beta is a measure of volatility). To understand the inherent weakness in this approach, one has to consider the difference between a publicly traded registered security, and a closely held unregistered (exempt from Securities Act of 1933 registration). In a publicly traded security, all shareholders have instant liquidity available, unless the stock is restricted temporarily for either a year or two years under applicable SEC rules.

It must be pointed out that what capitalization and discount rates represent is a measure of risk. When a security is unregistered, there are no active markets. From this evolved a theory that if a business sells at a cap rate of, say, 25% (the cap rate is merely the annual return on invested capital) and if the cost of money factor was assumed to be 5%, then the risk or amortization factor would be the difference, or 20%. At that rate the investor would receive a pre-tax return of the initial investment in five years (20% per year), and cover the 5% cost of money as well.

Using this concept, we can determine a defensible equity risk premium which is added to the risk free rate. Because the beta factor and industry risk factors are already contained in the market derived discount rates, what is left is to adjust for size, and for company specific risk.

The size adjustment is based upon the observation that risk is diminished with size. Or put another way, investment in very small companies is riskier than much larger ones, and therefore the earnings multiples are greater for larger ones.

The last adjustment that must be made is for what is called "specific company risk." This is nothing more than determining if the subject company is more or less risky than the average from marketplace comparisons.

Adjusting the element amortization periods to reflect the strengths and weaknesses of the subject. This will provide the basis for determining MVIC by the Income Approach using adjusted market discount rates.

SAMPLE COMPANY, INC.			
INCOME APPROACH USING MARKET CAPITALIZATION/DISCOUNT RATES			
CALCULATION OF MVIC			
		AVG FROM	APPRAISER'S
AMORTIZATION AND CAPITALIZATION RATE ANALYSIS		COMPS	ASSESSMENT
Adjustments To Amortization (Risk) Rate	Weight	Years To Amortize	
Lease Terms	6%	2.2	2.4
Relocatability	3%	2.2	1.0
Location	6%	2.2	2.4
Key Management Stability	6%	2.2	2.5
Non-Owner Management In Place	6%	2.2	2.5
Labor Availability	5%	2.2	2.2
Revenue Growth	10%	2.2	2.5
Relative Profitability (EBITDA/Sales)	10%	2.2	2.5
Customer Base Diversity	7%	2.2	2.5
Pending Litigation	20%	2.2	0.3
All other Factors	21%	2.2	2.2
Average Total Risk Rate Amortization	100%	2.2	1.9
Average Multiple from Market Comps		2.23	
VALUATION BY INCOME APPROACH - MARKET CAP RATES			
APPLICATION OF CAPITALIZATION RATE		Capitalization Rates	
		FROM	ADJUSTED
Risk Rate Factor Adjustment		COMPS	FROM
Aggregate Capitalization Rate*		44.87%	51.75%
Cost of Funds (20-Yr T-Bond + 3.25%)		5.64%	5.64%
Risk Premium Factor		39.23%	46.11%
Earnings Multiplier Unadjusted for EBITDA Size		2.23	1.93
Size Premium/Discount		1.80	1.80
Adjusted Capitalization Rate		24.93%	28.75%
Adjusted Earnings Multiplier (Inverse of Cap. Rate)		4.01	3.48
Capitalized Value of EBITDA (MVIC)		10,393,655	9,012,719

MVIC by Excess Earnings Approach

The Excess Earnings Analysis serves two purposes. It enables determination of the "goodwill" value by the Excess Earnings Method promulgated by IRS Revenue Ruling 68-609, and it also serves as a basis for a feasibility check on values found by other means.

The excess earnings analysis is an approach developed in IRS Rev Ruling 68-609. It is used to determine the value of intangible assets. In this case, the EBITDA is used as a basis, not SDE as the SDE used was appropriate only for determination of the value of the fixed plus intangible assets. The capitalization rate that was applied was inferred from comparative market transactions only, and does not reflect adjustments for specific company risk, which are developed in the valuation by the income approach. Thus it shows a generic value based upon industry comparables. While it is a good cross check, it is not deemed as reliable or relevant of the valuation of the MVIC by either the Market or Income Approach.

An example of a simplified excess earnings analysis is shown below. It uses EBITDA as a datum, and assumes a five year amortization for fixed assets. Based upon this a portion of the earnings are allocated to the fixed assets. The remaining earnings (excess earnings) is capitalized using the discount rates found in the comparative analysis to determine the intangible asset value.

It may be interesting to note that this approach was first used after Prohibition was enacted to determine the intangible asset value lost in the liquor industry due to the statute.

It is a crude approach compared to other modern approaches, but as before mentioned, it serves as a reasonable cross check.

SAMPLE COMPANY, INC.		
EXCESS EARNINGS APPROACH		
CALCULATION OF MVIC		
Weighted Average EBITDA		2,591,101
Estimated FMV of Fixed & Other Assets		5,807,377
Required Return on Assets:	Rate	Amount
Return on Investment	5.64%	
Amortization, %	20.00%	
Total Cap Rate for Fixed Assets	25.64%	
EBITDA Allocated To Fixed Assets		1,489,011
Excess Earnings		1,102,090
Capitalization Rate for Intangible Assets:		
Return on Investment	5.64%	
Adjusted Risk Rate Factor	23.11%	
Total Cap Rate Intangibles	28.75%	
Capitalized Value of Intangibles (Goodwill)		3,833,438
Estimated FMV of Fixed & Other Assets		5,807,377
Calculated Total MVIC		9,640,815

MVIC by Income Approach Using Ibbotson's Data

Ibbotson's SBBI Valuation Yearbook publishes data on market results for Stocks, Bonds, Bills and Inflation. From these tables data for the applicable Risk Free Rate, Equity Risk Premium, Size Premium and Industry Risk Premium can be taken. What is not provided is the Company Specific Risk Premium (Unsystematic Risk) which must be determined by the appraiser. In this valuation the same analysis as for the market discount rates is used, and is the difference in the discount rates after adjustment for company specific factors, prior to the application of the size premium for market discount rates, to determine the appropriate equity risk premium. The advantage of use of the Ibbotson's data is that it provides an estimated total equity risk premium based upon a broad base of public company data, plus the application of the company specific risk premium. The disadvantage is that these are derivative data, and not taken from specific market comparisons based upon the appraiser's judgment as to relevance. Therefore the discount rates derived from use of the Ibbotson's approach are probably less defensible than those taken directly from market transaction comparisons and/or income analysis. But they are worthy of consideration.

The company specific risk component of the Ibbotson's approach and be adjusted to reflect either a premium in value or a discount based upon an analysis of the subject company. Once this is applied correctly, valuation by the Ibbotson's data Income Approach should not be too disparate with that found by other means.

SAMPLE COMPANY, INC.	
INCOME APPROACH USING IBBOTSON'S BUILD-UP METHOD	
CALCULATION OF MVIC	
SIC Code: Coating, Engraving and Allied Services	347
Ibbotson's Input Data	
Risk Fee Rate (20-Year Treasury Bond)	2.39%
Equity Risk Premium	6.62%
Size Premium	0.121
Industry Risk Premium	7.52%
Estimated Company Specific Risk Adjustment (Unsystematic)	0.88%
After-Tax Net Cash Flow Discount Rate	29.47%
Capitalization Rate Calculation	
Long-Term Sustainable Growth Rate	3.00%
After-Tax Net Cash Flow Capitalization Rate for the Next Year	26.47%
Adjustment to Current Year	1.03
After-Tax Net Income Capitalization Rate for Current Year	25.70%
Cash to Earnings Factor (Included in Company Specific Risk)	n/a
Intangible Earnings Factor (Included in Company Specific Risk)	n/a
After-Tax Intangible Capitalization Rate for the Current Year	25.70%
Pre-Tax Net Cash Flow Capitalization Rate	
Weighted Average Actual Tax Rate (from Ibbotsons)	16.00%
Average Effective Tax Effect [1-Tax Rate]	84.00%
Pre-Tax Net Cash Flow Capitalization Rate for the Current	***30.59%***
Adjusted Earnings Multiplier (Inverse of Cap. Rate)	**3.27**
Capitalized Value of EBITDA (MVIC)	**8,469,431**

MVIC From Pratt's Public Company M&A Database

For larger privately held companies it is useful to also to determine MVIC using Merger and Acquisition data from public companies. This data is now provided as part of the Pratt's Stats system. It reflects M&A transactions of over 2900 public companies which are not traded on the exchanges. Therefore they more closely emulate closely held company transactions.

The analysis starts by computing the weighted averages for

key parameters, based upon the 0-5 weighting system discussed previously in this report. The raw ratio of EBITDA to MVIC is next adjusted using a factor for company specific risk determined in the Investment Analysis. Then a size adjustment is made based upon Ibbotson's SBBI data which is designed to reconcile size premium data from public companies as set forth in its SBBI Valuation Yearbook to subject companies based upon relative size of MVIC. This provides a discount rate. The discount rate is then converted

COMPANY	DESCRIPTION	SIC	REVS	EBITDA	MVIC	MVIC / EBITDA	EBITDA / REV	SALE TYPE	SALE DATE	WT
LeaRonal, Inc.	Manufactures Specialty Chemical Additives used by the Circuit Board, Connector, and Semiconductor Industries	3471	241,697	32,995	409,009	12.40	0.137	Stock	1/25/1999	2
WEIGHTED AVERAGES			241,697	32,995	409,009	12.40	0.137			2
SUBJECT			17,784	2,591			0.146			t

to a capitalization rate by subtracting the long term growth rate assumption which comes from industry data or the appraiser's analysis. These calculations and the resulting value are displayed in the table below. In the example shown, only one suitable comparison was found, but the illustration shows what data is available and how it was treated.

MVIC Using Guideline Public Company Comparisons

For the larger privately held companies useful inferences can be drawn from comparisons with publicly held companies in the same or similar industries. To do this, price to cash flow (or other benefit stream) ratios must be adjusted for the subject to reflect the differences between public and private valuation. The other that factors need to be addressed as set forth below:

Starting Discount Rate. The discount rate based upon the ratio of EBITDA to MVIC from the weighted average of selected Guideline Public Company comparisons is used as a starting point. The selections are weighted by using heuristic methodology. They are not random subsets therefore statistical analysis would not be appropriate. They are picked for perceived relevance, with the profitability (EBITDA to Revenues being of paramount importance. The relevancy of business types within the SIC code is also considered. This ratio is the raw discount rate, and will be adjusted by the following:

Specific Company Risk. First a determination of specific company risk (non-systemic risk) must be made. This analysis essentially determines the premium or discount to the discount rate that appropriately reflects the subject company's strengths and weaknesses when compared to the industry averages. The specific company risk is determined by performing a qualitative analysis of the subject, applying heuristics methodology, and determining an appropriate adjustment to the discount rate either found by an analysis of market comps, or by using an assumption of a starting 5 year amortization, and adjusting for the premium or discount warranted for the subject company.

Size Premium. The next adjustment is for size. Discount rates decrease with the increase of Market Capitalization theoretically reflecting less risk. In this valuation the size premium appropriate to the weighted average market capitalization (MVIC) for the selected guideline public companies is found. Next an approximate MVIC value for the subject company is estimated. The respective size premia factor for each is taken from Ibbotson SBBI, Table C-1, published by Morningstar, and the difference is applied as an adjustment to the discount rate.

Growth Rate. If the value is to be reported in *nominal dollars (not inflation adjusted)* a factor for estimated future inflation needs to be included in the estimated long term growth rate. Because this is already included in historic data, this valuation will use an estimate for growth including both a factor for organic growth, and a factor for the expected inflation rate. The estimated growth rate is important to determine the appropriate capitalization rate, which is expressed as the discount rate minus the long term growth rate.

BUSINESS DESCRIPTION	TICKER	REV	EBITDA	MARKET CAP	WT	EBITDA / REV	MKT CAP / REV	MKT CAP / EBITDA
Environmental Infrastructu	XMCP	1,377	-1,558	63	1	-1.13	0.05	-0.04
Handy & Harman	WXCO	662,015	72,516	189,068	3	0.11	0.29	2.61
Material Sciences	MASC	131,042	14,954	92,988	2	0.11	0.71	6.22
Ncoat	NCOA	6,033	-909	34	1	-0.15	0.01	-0.04
Propell Corporation	PROP	110	-1,095	455	1	-9.93	4.12	-0.42
AVERAGES		160,115	16,782	94,217	8	-1.33	0.81	2.47
SUBJECT		17,784	2,591			0.15		

PITCHBOOK GUIDELINE PUBLIC COMPANY DATA MARKET CAP ($000)	
Comparative MVIC Multiplier (Mkt Cap/EBITDA)	2.47
Comparative Capitalization Rate (1/Multiplier)	0.405
Estimated Company Specific Risk	0.038
Size Premium of Comps	0.092
Size Premium of Subject	0.121
Effective Size Premium Differential	0.029
Long Term Grow th Rate	0.03
EBITDA Capitalization Rate	**0.442**
Capitalized Value of EBITDA (Market Cap)	**5,861**

MVIC by Discounted Cash Flow Analysis

Where historic income is not considered representative of future performance, or where the data is scarce, a valuation can be performed using the discounted cash flow method. This determines the Present Value of a series of projected net cash flows. This approach requires discounting by years up to the point where stability is reached, and then determining a terminal value to the last year's projected net income by using the capitalization rate. This is then discounted from the final year to the present value and added to the present values for each year determined. The capitalization rate is related to the discount rate by the equation Cap Rate = Discount Rate minus Long Term Growth Rate.

Discounted Cash Flows are inherently flawed because most often projections are overly-optimistic. (Nobody ever projects a declining cash flow). To deal with this a discount rate must be applied that not only reflects the "static" discount rate that would be applied to an existing current operation to capitalize earnings, but must also reflect the additional risk that exists because the projected cash flow is a hypothetical event, and may never materialize.

To determine the appropriate discount rate takes a good bit of skill and experience.

Street-Smart Tip

A discounted cash flow analysis for valuation is dependent on *pre-tax* net operating cash flow (EBITDA).

For strategic planning what is of interest is the *after-tax* cash flow and balance sheet including calculations for real depreciation and taxes and capital requirements.

Internal Rate of Return (IRR)

The Internal Rate of Return is merely a financial calculation taught in business schools. It is derived by calculating the discount rate where the present value of the capital outflows equals that of the cash inflows using that discount rate. It is done manually by iterations. It is done by computers by pre-programmed iterations (like in Excel). What does that tell you about the value of a company or an asset? Absolutely nothing. Here is why.

This particular financial exercise was developed initially to attempt to compare the efficacy of acquiring one piece of equipment over another, assuming the same rate of inflows—where the inflows themselves were one of the assumptions. It was never intended to be used where there are disparate inflows.

If it is used to try to compare alternative business investments what is grandly missing is any kind of attempt at assessing the risk in each cash flow projection (the inflows). One projection may be conservative, another pie in the sky. Most people I have encountered in the world of finance cannot really explain why the IRR is of any value, but they often talk about comparative IRRs as if they are decisive determinants of which alternative has the most potential.

Are there any uses? Yes and no. They are fine for evaluating situations where the inflow is stipulated, such as projected manufacturing income from a particular type of machine. The IRR is used a lot in evaluating real estate developments where the cash flows can be projected with more certainty. But to compare, say five, different startup situations without any determination of the relative risks would be an exercise in self-deception.

In lieu of determining an IRR, wouldn't it be better to derive a Net Present Value with a discounted cash flow projection that takes into account the relative risk? If this is done for several alternatives, the NPV will show the comparative values in a more defensible way.

MVIC By Replacement Cost Approach

Use of the replacement cost approach is usually reserved for situations wherein the value cannot be determined from the market and income approaches: typically recent startups that have not reached representative operational cash flows, or for companies that have negative earnings. The replacement value can incorporate intangible asset value, even if the company is not profitable, based upon an analysis of intangible assets. When used, the approach excludes real estate, which is handled separately on the balance sheet and is not included in the definition of MVIC.

Putting It All Together – Reconciliation of MVIC

After using a number of approaches to determining MVIC, a final heuristic weighting is done to reflect the perceived relative reliability and credibility of the various approaches. If an asset valuation is all that is required you are nearly done. Just reconcile what other assets need to be included in the proposed acquisition. Things like inventory, receivables, and even some limited liabilities might be included in this.

If it is an equity valuation, then the next step is to restate the balance sheet, bringing all the assets for market value. This is done by subtracting the Fixed Assets from MVIC and showing the difference as Intangible Assets. If there are Discrete Intangible assets, this may be a bit more complicated and we will discuss that in a following section.

SAMPLE COMPANY, INC. APPRAISER'S OPINION OF VALUE ($000) MVIC		
		Weight
MVIC Based Upon Market Comparisons Approach	5,774	2
MVIC Based Upon Income Approach Using Market Cap/Discount Rates	9,013	5
MVIC Based Upon Income Approach Using Ibbotson's Equity Risk Premium	8,469	4
MVIC Based Upon Excess Earnings Analysis	9,641	1
MVIC Based Upon Replacement Value Analysis	N/A	0
MVIC Based Upon Discounted Cash Flow Analysis of Projected Earnings	N/A	0
MVIC Based Upon Pratts Public Co M & A Transactions Analysis	N/A	0
MVIC Based Upon PitchBook Guideline Public Company Analysis	5,861	3
Appraiser's Opinion Of MVIC	7,848	15
Capitalization Rate Based on Opinion of Value	0.33	
Multiplier Based on Opinion of Value	3.03	
(weighting is 0 - 5 based upon appraiser's judgment of relevance)		

Adjusting the Balance Sheet to Market Value

The final step in an equity valuation is to adjust the balance sheet from book value to fair or fair market value. This is not a balance sheet used for accounting, but only for valuation. It is common sense. If all the assets and liabilities of a company are shown at market value, then the equity will be at market value. The cash or equivalent items, which include cash, receivables and merchandise inventory. Receivables should show an allowance for bad debts based upon the bad debt history. Inventory should be reconciled, especially if the company is operating on a running inventory. It may require a physical inventory. But most important with inventory is to include only that which will be acceptable to a buyer. Over time many most companies have inventory that is either obsolete or damaged. In some cases it has been written off, but the merchandise is still physically present.

Fixed assets should be shown at market value. If depreciated book value is considered a good proxy for market value, then it can be used. If not, machinery and equipment must be separately appraised. For valuation purposes it is not too important the valuation of the fixed assets be "precise" therefore most often depreciated book value is used "as is." The reason for this is that to make the adjustment for the newly found MVIC the fixed assets are deducted from MVIC leaving the value of intangible assets which will be entered on the adjusted balance sheet. Since the total MVIC will not be changed, an understatement of the value of fixed assets results in a corresponding overstatement of intangible asset value, and vice versa.

Real estate, if owned by the company is appraised separately and shown as a separate line item adjusted to market value.

The only fly in the ointment occurs if the company has non-discrete intangible asset value – transferable Intellectual Property and the like. If the IP is licensed outside the company it must be separately appraised. If it is used totally internally, it can be valued by several approaches too complicated to go into here. Suffice it to say this needs to be addressed, usually by an analyst with the skills and experience to appraise it.

Liabilities must also be adjusted if there are credible contingent liabilities. Two common problem areas are health care contingent liabilities, and environmental remediation contingent liabilities.

The result will be a balance sheet that shows the assets and liabilities at market value (fair value or fair market value) and enables the calculation of the value in excess of book for the assets section, and the value in excess of par for the equity section.

SAMPLE COMPANY, INC.
BALANCE SHEET
December 31, 2011

	AT BOOK VALUE	ADJUSTED TO MARKET VALUE
ASSETS:		
Current Assets		
Cash and Cash Equivalents	3,301,356	3,301,356
Accounts Receivable	2,897,293	2,897,293
Investments - Marketable Securities	248,254	248,254
Income Tax Receivable	36,523	36,523
Prepaid Expenses	353,996	353,996
Inventory	783,216	783,216
Total Current Assets	**7,620,638**	**7,620,638**
Fixed Assets		
Property, Plant And Equipment (Excl Real Estate)		
Equipment and Leasehold Improvements	16,919,324	16,919,324
Less Accumulated Depreciation	-11,218,938	-11,218,938
Net Book Value Fixed Assets	5,700,386	5,700,386
Total Fixed Assets (Excl Real Estate)	**5,700,386**	**5,700,386**
Real Estate		
Land		N/A
Improvements		N/A
Total	0	N/A
Less Accumulated Depreciation	0	N/A
Appraised Value of Real Estate	N/A	
Total Real Estate	**0**	**0**
Other Assets		
Deferred Taxes		0
Deposits	40,994	40,994
Other Assets	65,997	65,997
Less Accumulated Amortization		0
Total Other Assets	**106,991**	**106,991**
Intangible Assets		
Discrete Intangible Assets (Intellect. Property)	0	N/A
Non-Discrete Intangible Assets (Goodwill) at Book		N/A
Less Accumulated Amortization		N/A
Appraised Value of Discrete Intangibles (IP)	N/A	
Appraised Value of non-Discrete Intangibles (Goodwill)	N/A	2,147,270
Total Intangible Assets	**0**	**2,147,270**
TOTAL ASSETS	**13,428,015**	**15,575,285**
Market Value in Excess of Book		**2,147,270**

82

SAMPLE COMPANY, INC. BALANCE SHEET December 31, 2011		
	AT BOOK VALUE	ADJUSTED TO MARKET VALUE
LIABILITIES		
Current Liabilities		
Accounts Payable	804,349	804,349
Current Portion of Capital Lease Obligation	4,163	4,163
Accrued Employee Compensation	160,439	160,439
Accrued Employee Vacation	280,479	280,479
Other Current Liabilities	483,811	483,811
Contingent Liability for Health Care Costs	0	1,210,094
Total Current Liabilities	**1,733,241**	**2,943,335**
Long Term Liabilities		
Capital Lease Obligations	3,655	3,655
Deferred Rent Payable	33,300	33,300
Deferred Tax Liability	1,206,647	1,206,647
Total Long Term Liabilities	**1,243,602**	**1,243,602**
TOTAL LIABILITIES	**2,976,843**	**4,186,937**
EQUITY		
Preferred Stock		0
Common Stock, no Par Value	293,923	293,923
Less Cost of Treasury Stock		0
Additional Paid-In Capital		0
Net Income		0
Retained Earnings	10,157,249	10,157,249
Adjustment for Contingent Health Care Costs		-1,210,094
Adjustment for Contingent ESOP Redemptions.		0
Value in Excess of Par	**0**	**2,147,270**
TOTAL EQUITY	**10,451,172**	**11,388,348**
TOTAL LIABILITIES & EQUITY	**13,428,015**	**15,575,285**

VALUATIONS AND APPRAISALS

Types of Valuations

Asset or Enterprise Valuations

If a sale of all of the assets of a private company is contemplated, as opposed to a stock sale, then an asset or enterprise valuation will be required. The enterprise value of a business is often called the Market Value of Invested Capital, or MVIC. It is essentially the sum of the value of the fixed operating assets (excluding real estate and discrete intangible assets such as IP) and non-discrete intangible assets – typically goodwill, covenants not to compete, etc. Other assets may be included in the sale, but they are usually cash-convertible assets such as merchandise inventory, and accounts receivable. These balance sheet items are not part of the enterprise value, but may be negotiated separately.

Real Estate owned by a company is always handled as a separate asset sale, usually in a separate escrow, because the transaction disclosure and reporting items are typically quite different than the requirement for the transfer of assets.

Early Stage Company Valuations

Early stage company valuations are normally required for two reasons:

- To establish a basis for negotiating capital contributions from investors, and

- To insure compliance with IRC 409A as regards issuance of incentive stock options to employees.

The valuation for these purposes can be combined. However the valuation for negotiating capital will require additional assessment analysis because it is based primarily upon assigning the correct risk discounts to a projected cash flow, and further to prepare a non-discounted cash flow projection for five years, with a running after tax cash balance, to determine that the burn rate does not exceed available capital.

Street-Smart Tip

Valuations for compliance with IRC 409A are crucial for two reasons:

- Tax compliance

- Avoiding shareholder litigation.

They most commonly value stock, membership interests, or partnership interests. Valuation of privately held partial interests usually involves application of discounts for lack of control and lack of marketability. Determination of the appropriate discounts can be a complicated process.

Discounts for Lack of Control and Marketability

All valuations are a valuation of an ownership interest. It is often referred to as a "bundle of rights." Normally direct ownership (fee interest in real estate) contains the most valuable bundle of rights, and lesser (derivative) forms such as ownership of a security interest, lease, license, or other such instrument will reduce the bundle of rights – and hence the value.

If the asset to be valued is a minority interest, and/or if it is subject to restricted marketability, and/or lack of control, appropriate discounts must also be applied.

Marketability Discounts. If an ownership suffers from reduced marketability, then a discount in value reflecting this is potentially applicable. However if the comparative data from which an inference of value is made is based upon market transactions which already represent any reduction of value for marketability, then an additional discount may not be warranted. For example, market transaction data from Pratt's Stats or BizComps represent non-registered, non-publicly traded, securities and the data already represents the effect in the market value for restricted marketability for a control interest. However if the basis of value is taken from derivatives from publicly traded transactions (i.e. Ibbotson's SBBI or Duff & Phelps) then additional discounts may be warranted. Further, marketability can also be reduced based upon restrictions on sales included by agreement. The relevant issues must be identified and quantified.

The standard for marketability is publicly traded securities, which convert to cash within three days. Closely held securities or direct ownership interests typically require from six months minimum up to several years to sell, and are subject reductions in value because of this.

Discounts for Lack of Liquidity. Liquidity is the measure of time it takes to convert an asset to cash. Marketability is the measure of time it takes to sell an asset. In technical terms, either or both can result in a loss of value, however for business valuations liquidity is usually included within, and as a part of, marketability unless otherwise specified.

Control Discounts. Over the years, business appraisers have adopted policies that separated the lack of control discount from the marketability discount. However, this appears to be a distinction without a difference as both are multiplicands of a total discount.

Discounts in General. Though the appropriateness of applying discounts is virtually universally accepted by the IRS and the valuation industry in general, recent court decisions have shown a fair amount of disagreement over the means of quantifying the appropriate discounts.

For the "marketability discount," because of a lack of actual data for partial interest transactions of exempt, non-registered, closely-held securities, appraisers have relied upon two principal sources of data from public company transactions: Initial Public Offering Studies, and Restricted Stock Studies to defend their discount opinion. As will be explained in the following paragraphs, these studies, while giving some information on discounts, are based upon sales of publicly traded securities or those that are about to become publicly traded.

The "standard" discount derived from these studies was typically 30% to 40%. Three cases against the Commissioner in 2003 found that such studies were not relevant to closely held private ownership. The reasons are fairly obvious:

Initial Public Offering Studies (IPO) shows the difference in the price of a stock before the offering and after, and infers that this is an appropriate marketability discount. This is an erroneous assumption for the following reasons:

Stock values of privately held companies typically are based upon *investment value* – that is an investor will be interested in both the current return, and the amortization factor (risk abatement factor) which will indicate how long it will take to recover his initial investment. This is necessary because of the high degree of illiquidity of non-public securities.

The IPO price, on the other hand, reflects a *speculative value* – that is, the investor is looking mainly towards price appreciation. By its nature once publicly traded, the stock should have high liquidity, so recovery of the investment is not a concern. Thus, this study is relevant only to companies anticipating an IPO. Unfortunately, these companies represent less than 1% of the companies extant in the U.S. In the period 1991-2000 the mean discounts ranged from 45% to 54%.

Restricted Stock Studies deal with stocks of public companies that have been *temporarily* restricted from sale for two years (later for one year) in the public markets (usually by virtue of securities regulations under rule 144). Nonetheless, there is no prohibition in selling these securities in private transactions, and they usually sell at an average of 30% or so less than publicly traded stock. But these are applicable only to publicly traded stocks which have only a temporary restriction from public markets, and not on the general "permanent" illiquidity problem faced with non-registered, exempt, closely-held securities which would make them far less marketable, and logically, less valuable. The studies do show that the discount increases with increases in the holding period. For a two year holding period the discounts averaged about 35%. In 1997, the SEC lowered the holding period to one year, and discounts dropped to about 25%.

Control discounts, (or more appropriately control-based marketability discounts) for small privately held companies are magnified in comparison with publicly held companies for a simple reason – in privately held companies the only practical way to recover the investment is liquidation (sale) of the company. Without control, an investor does not have the right to exercise this option. Thus minority interests in closely held companies are very difficult to sell. In practice, in the past appraisers have often attempted to base discounts for lack of control on control premium studies of public companies. The two are not the same at all. In the past a "standard" 35% discount has often been used, based upon public company data or valuation textbooks, without any analysis or other qualification. The lack of control in a closely held non-registered security causes even more reduction in value.

The case of Mandelbaum v. Commissioner, T.C.M 1995-255 determined that use of irrelevant data is unacceptable, and set forth some basic factors which might comprise the discount, but specified that this list was not exclusive, and other factors may apply as the situation dictates. It basically stated that an analysis must be done which is relevant to the subject. The factors listed to be evaluated included:

- Private vs. public sales of stock
- Financial statement analysis
- Dividend policy
- Nature of the company, history, position in the industry and economic outlook

- Management
- Amount of control in transferred shares
- Restrictions on transferability of stock
- Company's redemption policy
- Costs associated with making a public offering

IRS Revenue Ruling 77-287 deals with marketability discounts for "restricted securities", but it is silent on "exempted (unregistered) securities," which make up the vast majority of closely-held business securities.

The essence of the justification of significant discounts for minority interest in closely held securities is that they are inherently illiquid. There is virtually no published data available for four important reasons:

1. They normally are not sold to buyers outside of the subject business entity because of restrictions on such transactions. Thus the notion of a "public" market as contemplated by the definition of "fair market value" does not really exist in nature, it is hypothetical only.

2. Most business brokers cannot accept listings to sell closely held minority interests both because they are probably not licensed to do so, and/or are not insured with an E&O policy which permits them to do so. Business Brokers, licensed under state Real Estate Broker Licenses, can legally sell only 100% securities interests, but not partial interests. Partial interest securities sales normally require at least a FINRA Series 7 license, and the firm to be a broker dealer. Most broker-dealers are prohibited by their E&O insurance from dealing in exempt issues. The result is that there is virtually no professional marketing available.

3. In most cases, if a prospective buyer could be found, the costs and effort necessary to perform a due diligence investigation are not feasible for the buyer.

4. Arms-length sales of minority interests are extremely

rare, and there is no organized data source which tracks these transactions.

Intellectual Properties ("IP") are assets which are contained in the general category of Discrete Intangible Assets. But not all discrete intangibles are classified as Intellectual Property. Intellectual Property normally is property rights protected by law generally under the purview of the U. S. Patent and Trademark Office and/or the U.S. Copyright Office. They typically include Patents, Trademarks, Copyrights, and Trade Secrets. Trademarks are further protected by the Lanham Act to recover damages, profits and costs.

Domain Names (websites) for instance are technically not IP but often are treated similarly. They are intangible assets, and can be either a discrete or non-discrete asset depending on the use, the nature of the business they generate, and the brand identity. For instance a website like Amazon.com probably would have no value if the Amazon.com business were not sold with it. So it would be a non-discrete site and it would be valued as a business. Conversely, portal sites, such as Banks.com which offer some content, but primarily are a portal to advertisers, could be owned by anyone, and are discrete intangibles.

What Are Intangible Assets?

In general, all Intangible Assets fall into two principal categories:

1. "Discrete Intangible Assets" which have an independent legal existence and may be transferred independently from the overall business (i.e., intellectual properties such as patents, copyrights, royalties, trademarks, and trade secrets; franchise agreements, licenses, proprietary processes administrative policies and procedures).

2. "Non-Discrete Intangible Assets" are intangible assets which exist as part of the business enterprise itself, and cannot be sold separately (i.e., goodwill value and non-compete agreements)

The test to distinguish Discrete Intangibles from Non-Discrete Intangibles sets for the following criteria:

- Are they subject to specific identification and recognizable description;

- Are they subject to legal existence and protection;

- Are they subject to the right of private ownership, and is the private ownership legally transferable;

- Is there some tangible evidence that the asset exists;

- Have they been created or come into existence at an identifiable time or as the result of an identifiable event; and

- Are they subject to being destroyed or being terminated at an identifiable time or as the result of an identifiable event.

Importantly, Non-Discrete Intangible Assets cannot be sold effectively separate from the business enterprise and are typically included in the general category of "goodwill value." Of course, there are other types of non-discrete intangible assets including non-competition agreements, employment agreements, buy-sell agreements, customer lists, leases and certain licenses. The value of these non-discrete intangible assets lies in the principle that when all of the elements of a business system (capital, labor, management) are combined in a going-concern (or a potential going-concern), the value of the whole exceeds the sum of the value of the parts. From a valuation perspective, "goodwill" is that portion of assets that remains after the fair value of all the other assets is accounted for, including discrete intangibles. Importantly, goodwill is a quantifiable number, not just a "feeling" about the business, which is determined as part of a qualified professional valuation.

To determine the goodwill value, the following three elements are considered, though all three need not be present to create a goodwill value:

- The assets are in place and ready to use as a going-concern (capital, labor and management)

- There is excess economic income over that justifiably allocated to other assets; and/or

- There is an expectation of a valuable future event, such as gains on a sale.

Unless Non-Discrete Intangible Assets have a stream of profits that is separable and identifiable (e.g., a stream of royalty payments), they are typically analyzed as part of the going-concern value, rather than being valued separately. However, their presence can significantly influence the appraiser's analysis and judgment regarding the appropriate capitalization rate, which may result in a premium on value.

Reasons For Valuation

FASB Rules. For companies complying with GAAP accounting rules, intangible assets must be defined and allocated on the balance sheet in business combinations or acquisitions under FASB 141r. This requires a valuation of each identifiable intangible asset, such as IP, goodwill, covenants, beneficial licenses. Further, FASB 142 requires testing for impairment of intangible assets on an annual basis. If the value becomes impaired (i.e., declines) an adjustment for this is made on the balance sheet. However, it is not "written up" if the value increases. The impairment is taken as a charge in lieu of amortization. If the asset appreciates it will not be reflected until the time of sale and will then become part of the capital gains.

For companies which do not follow GAAP procedures (i.e., which include most non-public companies), the purchase price allocation is negotiated between the buyer and seller, and both sign an agreement which becomes part of their tax returns. This sets the basis for amortization or depreciation.

When a company owns IP, it is often incorrectly lumped into a general category of "intangible assets" and is not shown as a discrete intangible asset. For companies which acquire IP it should be shown at book acquisition cost as a discrete intangible asset. For companies which create their own IP, it should be shown at book creation cost. Ignoring this distinction may create a problem if a company becomes involved in litigation questioning the value of the IP, and the value is not shown as an asset on the company's balance sheet. The type of litigation may range from claims against an employee for breach of trade secrets, to patent infringement or diminution of value.

Sale or Merger. If a company is considering a merger or sale, it must know the value of its IP in order to satisfy due diligence requirements and negotiate effectively. This information may also be required to show evidence of ownership rights in a due diligence investigation.

Fairness Opinions. In most cases, a sale or merger will require an independent "fairness opinion" prepared by a qualified analyst, to determine the fairness of the terms for its client. This opinion is typically required under management's fiduciary responsibility to the company's shareholders.

If a public company is involved, while not officially mandated by the SEC, fairness opinions become a part of the disclosure statement (i.e., typically the S-4), which *is* mandated by the SEC.

To prepare a fairness opinion, the analyst must first value the securities of both parties. For public companies this is the question of "intrinsic value" vs. "market price" which must be resolved. Intrinsic analysis is valuation based upon fundamental economic characteristics, whereas market price may or may not reflect intrinsic value. In essence, market price is considered a less rational approach to value than intrinsic value.

The key to determining the intrinsic value of a company is to determine the fair value of its IP, if any exists.

Employee Incentive Stock Options.

Many companies that own IP often have employee incentive stock option programs in place. To avoid complicated and onerous tax consequences, a company issuing stock options needs to comply with the provisions of IRC 409A which basically holds that so long as options are issued with a strike price at or above the fair market value of the stock there will be no tax consequences to the issuer, and the employee will not be charged with current income. To comply with IRC 409A, a company needs a valuation which includes the value of all of the intangible assets.

What if IP is used only internally?

IP being created and used for internal purposes only is a very common situation. Under this circumstance, the company may not be able to determine which portion of its net income is attributable to internally generated and used IP. Nevertheless, the IP may still be valued by: 1) determining a reasonable royalty rate it would pay for use of the IP; 2) adjusting the cash flow downward to reflect this as an expense; and 3) capitalizing the anticipated royalties to determine the value of the IP. The value of the IP is then added to the balance sheet as a discrete intangible asset. For purposes of valuation, it is assumed that if the IP were sold, the company would obtain a license for use from the buyer as a condition of the sale. That said, this does not change the book value accounting used for tax purposes.

How are Reasonable Royalty Rates Determined

Reasonable royalty rates can be determined in multiple ways. There are several databases available which show rates paid for various types of IP. Access is relatively expensive. It is the appraiser's job to analyze them, and to attempt to derive the most defensible rate from this data. Often situations arise where a company has licensed its IP to another person/company at a rate either higher or lower than a "reasonable rate" for business reasons. Does this bind the company to that rate? No, it does not.

CAPITAL SOURCES

Private Equity

Friends and Family

The normal source of formation funding is the entrepreneur, his family and friends. Sometimes debt is involved, and sometimes the principal owner's 401k funds are invested. However this is not likely to produce near enough capital for significant growth.

Angel Investors

An angel investor is an typically affluent individual who provides capital for a business start-up, usually in exchange for convertible debt or ownership equity. A small but increasing number of angel investors organize themselves into angel groups or angel networks to share research, provide exposure to possible investment candidates, and pool their investment capital. Many groups also provide consulting support and training for start-up companies that they invest in.

The term "angel" originally comes from Broadway where it was used to describe wealthy individuals who provided money for theatrical productions. It has since morphed into use by entrepreneurs raising seed capital in the USA, and is now a generally accepted term world-wide.

Angel investors are often retired entrepreneurs or executives, who may be interested in angel investing for reasons that go beyond pure monetary return. Often they are associated with larger private equity groups, who are likely candidates for purchase once an investment hits critical mass. Many want to stay abreast of new innovations in a particular industry that they may find of use for other purposes. Thus, in addition to funds, angel investors can often provide valuable management advice and important contacts. Because there are no public exchanges listing their securities, private companies meet angel investors in several ways, including referrals from the investors' trusted sources and other business contacts; at investor conferences and symposia; and at meetings organized by groups of angels where companies pitch directly to investor in face-to-face meetings.

The number of individuals in the US who are believed to be actively involved in angel investing is in the order of 600,000. Many belong to angel groups with the goal of sharing deal flow and due diligence work, and pooling their funds to make larger investments. Angel groups are generally local organizations made up of 10 to 150 angel investors. Currently there are an estimated 300+ angel groups operating in the U. S.

Angels typically invest their own funds, unlike venture capitalists who manage the pooled money of others in a professionally-managed fund. The actual entity that provides the funding may be a trust, business, limited liability company, investment fund, or other vehicle controlled by the angel. Because of both the financial strength and business savvy provided by angels, ventures funded by angels have the lowest rate of failure of all forms of financing.

Angel capital fills the gap in start-up financing between "friends and family who provide seed funding and formal venture capital. Although it is usually difficult to raise more than a few hundred thousand dollars from friends and family, most traditional venture capital funds are usually not interested in investments under $2 million. Thus, angel investment is a common second round of financing for high-growth start-ups, and accounts in total for almost as much money invested annually as all venture capital funds combined, but the investments are made into more than 60 times as many companies. The total annual investments are estimated at in excess of $20 billion in over 60,000 companies.

There is no minimum or maximum amount for angel investors, and the range can go anywhere from a few thousand, to a few million dollars. In a large shift from 2009,

Angel financing, while more readily available than VC financing, is still difficult to raise and requires very thorough preparation to make a successful pitch. However some new models are developing that are trying to make this easier.

Angel Investment profile

Angel investments face high risk and are potentially subject to dilution from future investment rounds. Therefore they require a very high return on investment. Because a large percentage of angel investments are lost completely when early stage companies fail, professional angel investors typically seek investments that have the potential to return at least 10 or more times their original investment within 5 years, through a defined exit strategy, such as plans for an initial public offering or a sale to private equity. Some angels require even higher returns, looking for companies that will have at least the potential to provide a 20x-30x return over a five- to seven-year holding period.

In the United States Silicon Valley dominates angel funding with about 40% of the market. In the United States, angels are generally qualified as "accredited investors" as defined by the Securities Act of 1933 which makes SEC exempt sales of securities possible under Regulation D.

In the UK there are an estimated 6,000 angel investors with an average investment size of about $65,000 U.S.D.

Venture Capital

Venture capital (VC) is financial capital provided to early-stage, high risk, high potential growth startup companies. The venture capital fund profits by owning equity in the companies it invests in, which usually have a unique technology or business model in high-technology industries, such as biotechnology, IT, software, etc. The typical venture capital investment occurs after the seed funding round with an objective of generating a profit through an eventual capital event, such as an IPO or sale of the company.

In addition to angel investing and other seed funding options, venture capital is attractive for new companies with limited operating history that are too small to raise capital in the public markets and have not reached the point where they are able to secure a bank loan or complete a debt offering. In exchange for the high risk that venture capitalists assume by investing in smaller and less mature companies, venture capitalists usually get significant control over company decisions, in addition to a significant portion of the company's ownership.

Every year, there are nearly 2 million new businesses created in the USA, and approximately one-third obtain venture capital or angel financing. Obtaining venture capital is substantially different from raising debt or a loan from a lender. Lenders have a legal right to interest on a loan and repayment of the capital, irrespective of the success or failure of a business. Venture capital is invested in exchange for an equity stake in the business. As a shareholder, the venture capitalist's return is dependent on the growth and profitability of the business. This return is generally earned when the venture capitalist "exits" by selling its shareholdings when the business is sold to another owner.

Venture capitalists are typically very selective in deciding what to invest in; as a rule of thumb, a fund typically will invest in less than 1% of opportunities presented to it. VC funds are most interested in ventures with exceptionally high growth potential, as only such opportunities are likely capable of providing the financial returns and successful exit event within the required timeframe (typically 3–7 years) that venture capitalists expect.

Because VC investments are illiquid and require the extended timeframe to harvest, venture capitalists normally complete thorough due diligence prior to investment.

Private companies meet venture capital firms and other private equity investors in several ways, including referrals from the investors' trusted sources and other business contacts; investor conferences; and summits where companies pitch directly to investor groups in face-to-face meetings, including a variant known as "Speed Venturing", which is akin to speed-dating for capital, where the investor decides within 10 minutes whether he wants a follow-up meeting. In addition, there are some new private online networks that are emerging to provide additional opportunities to meet investors.

This need for high returns makes venture funding an expensive capital source for companies, and most suitable for businesses having large up-front capital requirements, which cannot be financed by cheaper alternatives such as debt. That is most commonly the case for intangible assets such as software, and other intellectual property, whose value is unproven. In turn, this explains why venture capital is most prevalent in the fast-growing technology and life sciences or biotechnology fields.

Venture Capital Financing Stages

There are five common stages of venture capital financing:

1. The Seed stage
2. The Start-up stage
3. The Second stage
4. The Third stage
5. The Bridge/Pre-public stage

The number and type of stages may be extended by the VC firm if it deems necessary. This may happen if the venture does not perform as expected due to bad management or adverse market conditions.

There are typically six stages of venture round financing offered in Venture Capital, that roughly correspond to the above listed stages of a company's development.

- Seed funding: Low level financing needed to prove a new idea, often provided by angel investors. Crowd funding is also emerging as an option for seed funding.

- Start-up: Early stage firms that need funding for expenses associated with marketing and product development

- Growth (Series A round): Early sales and manufacturing funds

- Second-Round: Working capital for early stage companies that are selling product, but not yet turning a profit. (Frequently Series B and C rounds, etc.)

- Expansion : Also called Mezzanine financing, this is expansion money for a newly profitable company

- Exit of venture capitalist : Also called bridge financing, 4th round is intended to finance the "going public" process

Between the first round and the fourth round, venture-backed companies may also seek to take venture debt.

Private Equity Funds

Both Venture Capital and Angel Investors are subsets of private equity. But not all private equity falls into those two groups. There are also funds, some quite large, that represent pooled and professionally managed private equity. Many of these funds do acquire entire businesses, and may be of interest for a sale, or for an exit strategy for a new venture.

Other Capital Sources

Leveraged Buy-out

A Leveraged Buyout (LBO) is an acquisition (usually of a

company but, can also be single assets such as a real estate property) where the purchase price is financed through a combination of equity and debt and in which the cash flows or assets of the target are used to secure and repay the debt. Since the debt, be it senior or mezzanine, always has a lower cost of capital than the equity, the returns on the equity increase with increasing debt. The debt thus effectively serves as a lever to increase returns which explains the origin of the term LBO.

LBOs are a very common occurrence in today's "Mergers and Acquisitions" (M&A) environment. LBOs can have many different forms such as Management Buy-out (MBO), Management Buy-in (MBI), secondary buyout and tertiary buyout, among others, and can occur in growth situations, restructuring situations and insolvencies. LBOs mostly occur in private companies, but can also be employed with public companies in a so-called PtoP transaction -- Public to Private.

As investors can increase their returns by employing a very high leverage (i.e., a high ratio of debt to equity), they have an incentive to employ as much debt as sustainable to finance an acquisition. This has in many cases led to situations, in which companies were over-leveraged, meaning that they did not generate sufficient cash flows to service their debt, which in turn led to insolvency or to debt-to-equity swaps in which the equity owners lose control over the business and the debt providers assume the equity.

LBOs have become very attractive as they usually represent a win-win situation for the investor and the banks: The financial sponsor can increase the returns on his equity by employing the leverage; banks can make substantially higher margins when supporting the financing of LBOs as compared to usual corporate lending, because the interest chargeable is much higher.

The amount of debt banks are willing to provide to support an LBO varies greatly and depends, among other things, on:

- The quality of the asset to be acquired

- The amount of equity

- The history and experience of the investor

- The economic environment

For companies with very stable and secured cash flows (e.g., real estate portfolios with rental income secured with long term rental agreements), debt volumes of up to 100% of the purchase price have been provided. In situations of "normal" companies with normal business risks, debt of 40–60% of the purchase price are normal figures. The debt ratios that are possible vary also significantly between the regions and between the industries of the target.

Depending on the size and purchase price of the acquisition, the debt is often provided as:

- Senior debt: This debt is secured with the assets of the target company and has the lowest interest margins

- Junior debt (usually mezzanine): This debt usually has no securities and bears thus a higher interest margins

In larger transactions, sometimes all or part of these two debt types is replaced by high yield bonds. Depending on the size of the acquisition, debt as well as equity can be provided by more than one party. In larger transactions, debt is often syndicated to reduce risk. Another form of debt that is used in LBOs are seller notes in which the seller effectively uses parts of the proceeds of the sale to grant a loan to the purchaser. Such seller notes are often employed in management buyouts or in situations with very restrictive bank financing environments. Note that in close to all cases of LBOs, the only securities available for the debt are the assets and cash flows of the company. The investor usually is not willing to provide other securities outside of the acquisition target as securities.

As a rule of thumb, senior debt usually has interest margins of 3–5% over Libor with a term of 5–7 years, junior debt has

margins of 7–16%, and needs to be paid back in one payment after 7–10 years. Junior debt often additionally has warrants.
[

Personal 401k Equity Investment

An opportunity exists for investors who have significant 401k investment trusts to invest all or part of that fund into a small business which they control. The contributed funds are a true equity investment, and the entity must normally be a "C-corporation." They are not a loan from the 401k. Therefore there is no taxable event upon creation of this financing structure so long as it is done properly. There are several firms in the U.S. that provide ministerial services to accomplish this.

There are "strings" to this investment, and the investor should be clear on what they are. Some incur costs. However, once invested the 401k's shares can be bought out at any time at fair market value. This will release the company from further compliance with ERISA.

In the alternative, the CEO could, at any time take a distribution of the stock held by the 401k to him personally. Of course this would subject him to income taxes and early withdrawal penalties attendant to any 401k.

This program can be a good source of equity capital, and generally costs less than an SBA loan, which is likely the only other feasible source for a small business.

The CEO of the company into which the CEO's pension trust funds are invested incurs two fiduciary responsibilities: one to his shareholders, and one to the pension trust. This creates an inherent conflict of interest, which can be mitigated so long as the CEO exercises appropriate steps to insure the preservation of value of the 401k investment precedes the profitability of the company, or compensation to the CEO.

The rules pertain to Qualified Pension Trusts issued under ERISA, including Employee Stock Ownership Plans (ESOPs) and directed 401(k) plans which are invested in private companies. Pursuant to ERISA the U. S. Department of Labor has set forth regulations which provide guidance for the Trustee to exercise due diligence and good faith in valuation of assets for which there is no active market. These regulations have been in the "proposed state" for several years, and though not officially adopted, the Department of Labor has directed that they be used until made final.

A key to investment of 401k funds in a private business is "adequate consideration." That is to insure that the pension trust obtains its investment interest at, or less, than Fair Market Value as determined by appraisal.

The Proposed Regulation 2510.318(b) and the proposed Regulation 29CFR2510.3-18 to ERISA expand on the definition of "adequate consideration," and though not yet formally adopted, the industry has adopted the criteria to use until enacted.

Under ERISA, "adequate consideration" means the fair market value of the asset as determined in good faith by the trustee or named fiduciary pursuant to the plan and in accordance with regulations promulgated by the Secretary of Labor.

The proposed regulation delineates the scope of this regulation by establishing two criteria, both of which must be met for a valid determination of adequate consideration.

First the value assigned to an asset must reflect its fair market value as determined pursuant to proposed § 2510.3-18(b) (2).

Second the value assigned to an asset must be the product of a determination made by the fiduciary in good faith as defined in proposed §2510.3-18(b) (3).

For the first criterion the definition of fair market value is set forth as:

"*...the price at which an asset would change hands between a willing buyer and a willing seller when the former is not under any compulsion to buy and the latter is not under any* *compulsion to sell, and both parties are able, as well as willing, to trade and are well-informed about the asset and the market for the asset."* (It should be noted that this definition is consistent with that adopted by most appraisal organizations, and is also consistent with IRS code and IRS Revenue Ruling 59-60, and the Uniform Standards for Professional Appraisal Practice.)

The second criterion sets forth the following:

- The valuation must be set forth in a written document, the "good faith" requirement establishes an objective standard of conduct, rather than an inquiry into the state of mind of the Trustee,

- the fiduciary making the valuation must itself either be independent of all the parties to the transaction or must rely on the report of an appraiser who is independent of all the parties,

- if donated property, the valuation should follow Rev. Proc 66-49 (IRS Revenue Ruling 83-20) which sets forth the format required by the IRS for valuation of donated property, or

- If the property is to be purchased, it requires that Revenue Ruling 59-60 shall apply. This documentation must contain, at minimum

  o A summary of the qualifications of the appraiser,

  o A statement of the asset's value and a statement of the methods used in determining that value, and the reasons used to determine the value,

  o A full description of the asset being valued

  o The factors taken into account in making the valuation, including any restrictions understandings, agreement or obligations limiting the use or disposition of the property, o The purpose for which the valuation was made,

o The relevance or significance accorded to the valuation methodologies taken into account,

o The nature of the business and the history of the enterprise from its inception

o The economic outlook in general, and the outlook for the specific industry in particular,

o The book value of the securities and the financial condition of the business,

o The earning capacity of the company,

o The dividend-paying capacity of the company,

o Whether or not the enterprise has goodwill or other intangible value,

o The market price of securities of corporations engaged in the same or a similar line of business (later expanded to include similar fee holdings),

o The marketability of the securities, or lack thereof,

o Whether or not the Seller would be able to obtain a control premium from a third party.

Compliance With ERISA and Proposed Regulations

The appraisal procedures and this resulting appraisal report have been done in strict compliance with the Uniform Standards for Professional Appraisal Practice, ("USPAP") Standards 9 and 10 which apply to Business Appraisal procedures, and Business Appraisal Reports, respectively. These standards require compliance meeting all of the criteria set forth under ERISA and the proposed additional regulations being promulgated hereunder. The findings and opinions contained in this report provide a basis for the

Trustee to determine "adequate consideration" and the fair market value of the assets held or being acquired by Qualified Pension Trusts.

SBA Loans

SBA loans are included only because they are often the only viable alternative for debt financing for many, if not most, small businesses. The SBA offers a number of special programs, but the basic loans for starting or expanding a business are:

7(a) Loan Program

This option provides for loans to eligible borrowers for starting, acquiring and expanding a small business. This type of loan is the most basic and the most used within SBA's business loan programs. Borrowers must apply through a participating lender institution.

The series 7 loans are straight business loans, usually at 2 ¾% over prime, variable rate loans. Maturities are 7 or 10 years. Though the SBA does not require collateral, but the banks that issue them usually do. Collateral usually takes the form a personal guarantee and a lien on the borrower's home. The loans are 80% guaranteed by the U. S. Government. Since they can charge market rates, banks which qualify as preferred lenders (means that they make their own underwriting decisions) like these loans because if structured carefully they have zero risk. Their risk essentially occurs if there is less than 20% equity in the transaction, and if they do not scrupulously comply with the SBA Standard Operating Procedure. The banks also charge points and a loan guarantee fee (insurance). These are not inexpensive loans.

Certified Development Company (CDC) 504 Loan Program

The 504 Loan provides growing businesses with long-term, fixed-rate financing for major fixed assets, such as land and buildings. Loans are collateralized by the assets.

Microloan Program

Offers very small loans to start-up, newly established or growing small business concerns. SBA makes funds available to nonprofit community based lenders which, in turn, make loans to eligible borrowers in amounts up to a maximum of $50,000. Applications are submitted to the local intermediary and all credit decisions are made on the local level.

The participating banks' policies vary widely, so if this form of financing is of interest it is necessary to contact a specific bank and request a loan. The bank will issue terms and conditions that they require to issue the loan.

Private Buyers/Seller Financing

Prior to the real estate collapse in 2008, most small business acquisitions were financed by a buyer borrowing against his home. This option has all but disappeared. Most prospective buyers do not have adequate equity to purchase a business outright. So this leaves a seller with the choice – he can either offer some seller financing in the form of a note, or probably preclude a sale of the business.

Over the years as a business broker, many, if not most, sellers I encountered were adamantly opposed to offering seller's financing. A seller's note secured with an all-encompassing personal guarantee is pretty powerful security if the buyer has significant personal assets. In my view it is better than a second trust deed on real estate, though you may want that too. If the loan is secured with the personal guarantee, foreclosure is made much simpler than for real estate, and if the business asset sold is included in the guarantee, then a foreclosing seller keeps the down payment, and goes after the buyer for the balance. He can either take back the business, or not, depending on the status of the business at the time. If the buyer has defaulted it is likely because he was unable to operate the business successfully.

Another aspect of seller financing is that the seller is often able to negotiate a much higher price. So while it is not headache free, it can be made viable by obtaining enough down payment and a suitable guarantee.

There are ways to combine several sources. For instance, if a prospective buyer has a 401k he can use those funds as equity. He can obtain an SBA loan so long as there is at least 20% equity in the business. Most banks will credit 80% or so of a seller's note, if subordinate to the SBA loan as equity. So out of the mix of possible sources it is often possible to structure a very safe and viable financing.

Use of the 401k equity approach does involve compliance issues with the Department of Labor. Some of the problems that arise are when the beneficiary of the 401k also owns real estate and wants to lease it to the company financed by the 401k. He can't do this under the "related party" provisions of ERISA. So either the real property has to be transferred to the company, as an asset as well, or an alternative has to be found.

Also the IRS and the Department of Labor appear to believe that equity in the company must be offered to all employees. In practical terms this probably should not be offered because investment in a minority interest in a C-corporation results in serious discount for lack of control and marketability, thus diminishing the pension trust's value. Some attorneys have been of the opinion that it is not required to offer company stock to the employees, but that they have a right to participate in the 401k plan – which would be invested in a managed trust. This sounds more reasonable, but again, this should be reviewed by an attorney.

ESOPS

The acronym "ESOP" is used in two different contexts, and means different things in each context. An Employee Stock Ownership Plan

is a provision under ERISA where the company can actually be sold to employees. An ESOP trust is set up which owns the stock, and the company can borrow money to purchase the stock, usually from founders. This provides an exit strategy for founders, and payoff of the loan is done though pension trust contributions. There is a whole body of law surrounding ESOPs of this type, and professional advisors are needed for many areas.

As second type of plan, also often referred to as an "ESOP" is an Employee Stock Option Plan. This is not part of ERISA, and is strictly a company plan to award options to purchase company stock. This is governed heavily by section 409A or the Internal Revenue Code. Unless this code is complied with, there are complicated tax ramifications that can arise, both for the employer and the employee.

If a company implements such a plan, it should be coordinated with its equity investors, because there is a potential for dilution if care is not taken. Again, professional advisors can protect against this.

THE STRATEGIC PLAN

For early stage high growth (or potential growth) companies the perceived credibility and comprehensiveness of the strategic plan is the principal determinant of risk – and hence value.

The so-called business plan, is usually the initial outline for a strategic plan. It is a schematic concept with little in the way of supporting documentation. As the business plan is developed over time it will morph into a complete strategic plan as serious analytic work is done to develop each element. The following list shows elements of a "typical" strategic plan. However each business has its own requirements, and the plan should be adjusted to accommodate them.

Elements of a Strategic Plan

- Vision Statement
- Mission Statement
- Management Team Profiles and Capability
- Market Analysis and Assessment
- Competitor Analysis
- Intellectual Property Consideration
- Target Customer Analysis
- Marketing Plan
- Risk Management Plan
- "Five Forces" Analysis (similar to but more advanced than SWOT)
- Capital Requirements Analysis
- Sources of Funding
- Staffing and Compensation Plan
- Tax Planning
- Operations Plan
- Pro Forma Income and Balance Sheet Projections
- Valuation

We will expand on these one-by-one.

Vision Statement. The vision statement clearly defines the goal. Without a vision statement, effective business planning would be impossible; it's the vision statement that provides the destination for the journey, and without a destination, how can you plan the route?

Mission Statement. The mission statement clearly sets forth the objectives to achieve the vision, and provides a basis for quantitative scoring to determine progress.

Management Team Profiles and Capability. The roles, strengths, weaknesses (gaps) and needs is analyzed with respect to the Mission Statement and operational needs.

Market Analysis and Assessment. Normally prepared by a firm with expertise in the industry and market segment. The goal is to attempt to identify the market opportunities, and if offering a new and innovative product, where it may generate new demand. It should also estimate absorption rates, from which the growth plan can be developed.

Competitor Analysis. This needs to be done exhaustively and objectively. It considers objective fact, as well as subjective aspects such as branding, market share and perceived value.

Intellectual Property Consideration. This must be done from several directions.

- First, a plan to develop and protect the company's own IP is required.

- Second, an analysis of "competing" IP must be made to determine infringement potential, and plans to deal with this.

- Third, if the company's IP is to be licensed to others, for profit, a plan for this needs to be developed and integrated into the profit projections.

Target Customer Analysis. This will involve surveys of potential, and perhaps existing customers, to determine acceptability of the proposed product, concerns, perceived advantages, etc., as well as which target customer segments appear to be the strongest potential.

Marketing Plan. This plan must not only identify how the product will be marketed, but contain estimates of cost of marketing. These costs must be separated into ongoing costs to be funded from sales, and capitalized costs which must be included in part of the capital requirements.

Risk Management Plan. Costs of insurance for insurable risks where these exist must be estimated. Risk mitigation plans for risks that are not insurable must be developed.

"Five Forces" Analysis (similar but more advanced than SWOT).

Capital Requirements Analysis. This has to be coordinated with other elements of the plan. Facilities needs should be planned. Capitalized funds for startup initiatives such as marketing and sales, product development and testing, etc. must be estimated. If the company plans for an IPO, much of this cost should be capitalized.

For more advanced companies a serious analysis of real depreciation of capital equipment should be done, and plans for funding the replacement developed. Too often depreciation is treated as a "tax gimmick" only, and no provision is made to replace obsolete equipment. Early stage companies often do not think that far ahead.

Staffing and Compensation Plan. Personnel needs must be

estimated. A compensation plan needs to be developed. If employee incentive options are planned to reduce current costs, and induce talent to join, these must not only comply with IRC 409A, they must be integrated with plans to obtain equity capital so that dilution aspects are resolved.

Tax Planning. Tax consequences of operations, and for capital events such as a sale to private equity must be analyzed. Likewise, the ramifications of an IPO. Compliance with IRC 409A should be evaluated to insure against unforeseen and unsought tax liabilities.

Operations Plan. In early state companies this is single policy statement. As companies become more complicated, each division and each department will require a plan.

Pro Forma Income and Balance Sheet Projections. This is the result of all the other segments put into a comprehensive financial plan. The object to show probable cash flows, and to track the effect on available working capital. This is the analysis that will shed light on the "burn rate" and whether or not the company has adequate capital. Run through a variety of scenarios and assumptions, it becomes the basis for a sensitivity analysis to determine critical elements for survival, such as sales, margins, costs and expenses.

Valuations. All companies have needs for valuations from time to time. They are needed to comply with IRC 409A for incentive options plans. They are needed for negotiating infusions of capital. They are needed for consideration of M & A opportunities. They are an unavoidable expense and a budget for them should be developed.

In the end, the company should be continuously aware of the market value of its equity, because that is the true measure of performance of management.

Sub-elements of the Strategic Plan

Each main element of the plan is composed of sub-elements which must be developed for each business. The permutations and combinations are far too numerous to explain here, but an example is given below for one category—Risk Management Plan, and one subsection of that – Risk Assessment. It shows some idea of the granularity with which the plan must be developed to be effective.

Sample Risk Assessment Checklist

Assumptions
Economic
Industry
Competitive
Availability of External Financing
Availability of Equity Financing

Major growth drivers and prospects
Organic
       Current Customer Growth
       Market Penetration
       Geographic Penetration
       Demographic Growth
Innovation
External Technology Platforms
Government/Regulation
Industry Standards
Tax Code
Acquisition

Currency & Pricing Risks
Foreign Operations
       Currency
       Government Regulation
       Cultural Factors
Industry and company pricing policies

Products
Description of each product
Major customers and applications
Historical and projected growth rates
Market shares
Speed and nature of technological change
Timing of new products, product enhancements
Cost structure and profitability

Customer Information
List of top 20 customers for the past two fiscal years
    (name, contact name, address, phone number, product(s) owned, and timing of purchase(s))
List of strategic relationships
    (name, contact name, phone number, revenue contribution, marketing agreements)
Revenue by customer
    (name, contact name, phone number for any accounting for 5 percent or more of revenue)
Brief description of any significant relationships severed within the last two

years.
>(name, contact name, phone number)

Supplier Information
List of top 20 suppliers for the past two fiscal years and current year-to-date with contact information
>(name, contact name, phone number, purchase amounts, supplier agreements)

List of strategic relationships
>(name, contact name, phone number, product contribution, contract agreements)

Expense by Supplier
>(name, contact name, phone number for any accounting for 5 percent or more of product cost)

Brief description of any significant relationships severed within the last two years.
>(name, contact name, phone number)

Competition
List of Direct Competitors
List of Indirect Competitors
Description of market scope by product line
Narrative of competitors by market segment including:
>Market position and related strengths and weaknesses as perceived in the market place
>Basis of competition (e.g., price, service, technology, distribution)

Substitute Products
List of Substitute Products and Producers

Potential New Entrants
List of Potential New Entrants and their Products

Marketing, Sales, and Distribution
Strategy and implementation
Discussion of domestic and international distribution channels
Positioning of the Company and its products
Marketing opportunities/marketing risks
Description of marketing programs
>Website
>Product Literature
>Email / Newsletter Campaigns
>Public Relations
>Press releases
>Advertising
>Social media

Pipeline analysis
Principal drivers for generating new business
Sales force productivity model
Compensation
Sales Cycle
Plan for New Hires

Ability to implement marketing plan with current and projected budgets

Branding
Names
Logo
Slogans
Trademarks, Copyrights
Brand Ability to Deliver Message
Brand's conflicting messages
Company practices vs. brand Image
Advertising
Social Media
Trade Shows
Events
Environmental & Philanthropy Initiatives
Managing for Brand value
Alignment vs. Competition

Research and Development
Description of R&D organization
Strategy
Key Personnel
Major Activities
New Product Pipeline
Length of Product development Cycle(s)
Status and Timing of key Projects
Cost of Development
Critical Technology Necessary for Implementation
Risks

Management and Personnel
Organization Chart
Historical and projected headcount by function and location
Summary biographies of senior management
        Employment history, age, service time, years in current position
        Synopsis of key employment agreements
Significant employee relations problems, past or present
Personnel Turnover Summary past three years
Benefit plans

Compensation & Incentive Compensation Plans
Goal Alignment
Retention of Star performers
Mitigate Inappropriate Risk-taking
Maximize Appropriate risk-taking
Compliance with industry/government regulations
Meet demands for disclosure form external regulators and stakeholders

Legal and Related Matters
Pending lawsuits against the Company
       claimed damages, brief history, status, anticipated outcome
Pending lawsuits initiated by Company
       claimed damages, brief history, status, anticipated outcome
Description of environmental and employee safety issues and liabilities
Safety precautions
New regulations and their consequences
List of material patents, copyrights, licenses, and trademarks (issued and pending)
Summary of insurance coverage/any material exposure
History of SEC or other regulatory agency problem, if any

INDEX

Adjusting the Balance Sheet..80
American Institute of Certified Public Accountants (AICPA).................................1
American Society of Appraisers (ASA...1
Angel Investors..96
Business Plan...17
CAPITAL SOURCES 96
Capitalization or Discount Rate...67
Comparative Ratio Analysis 60
Compliance With ERISA 107
Control discounts...88
Copyrights 56
discount rate.............................4, 7, 8, 9, 11, 12, 13, 14, 15, 16, 43, 60, 66, 67, 74, 75, 76, 77
Discounted Cash Flow Analysis 77
Discounts for Lack of Control and Marketability...85
EBITDA..10, 11, 12, 35, 49, 65, 67, 70, 74, 75
Elements of a Strategic Plan..112
Employee Incentive Stock Options 94
Employee Stock Ownership Plan 110
Excess Earnings Approach...70
Fair Compensation for Owner's Work 50
Fair Market Value...6
Fair Value 6
Fairness Opinions 93
Forced Liquidation Value..6
forensic financial analyst 60
Growth Rate..75
Guideline Public Company Comparisons..74
Heuristics...28
How is Risk Measured?...7
Ibbotson's Data..71
Income Approach..66
Institute of Business of Appraisers (IBA) 1
Intangible Assets..44, 79, 90, 91, 92
Internal Rate of Return 78
Intrinsic Value 6
Investment Value 6, 47
IP is used only internally 95
IPO..18, 19, 25, 87, 98, 114
Liquidation Value 6, 47
Mandelbaum v. Commissioner...88
Market Value 6
Mitigation of Risk..13
MVIC.............................9, 49, 62, 63, 64, 65, 68, 70, 71, 73, 74, 75, 77, 79, 81, 84
National Association of Certified Valuators and Analysts (NACVA)......................1

Negotiating 12
Non-Discrete Intangible Assets 91
Orderly Liquidation Value...6
Paying a Premium...11
Pratt's Public Company M&A Database 73
pre-money valuation 13, 23, 24, 26, 27
Private Buyers/Seller Financing 109
Private Equity 96, 101
Reasonable Royalty Rates 95
Reconciliation of MVIC 79
Replacement Cost Approach 79
Restricted Stock Studies 87
Round A...24
Round B 24
Royalties....57
Rules of Thumb 36
Sale or Merger...93
SBA Loans..107
SEC compliance..19
Self-Cancelling Errors 36
'Series A Financing' 25
Size Premium 71, 75
Specific Company Risk...75
Strategic Plan...17, 18, 112
Strategic Value..6
Street-Smart tips 4
street-smarts..4
Sub-elements of the Strategic Plan 115
The Bridge/Pre-public Stage..22
The Seed Stage 17
Theories of Risk..13
Uniform Standards of Professional Appraisal Practice 44
USPAP 4, 44, 45, 46, 107
Value..............................2, 3, 6, 10, 15, 30, 33, 41, 43, 46, 47, 48, 61, 62, 65, 67, 77, 84, 105
Venture Capital..98
What Are Intangible Assets 90

ABOUT THE AUTHOR

Gerald W. Barney began his career as a financial professional in 1971 as a securities broker with the regional firm Mitchum, Jones & Templeton (later acquired by Paine Webber) dealing in mid-sized mergers and acquisitions and commercial real estate syndications. Since 1983 he has been active principally in providing financial services to private business, including, valuation, consulting, brokerage and financing. During his career in financial services he has served as CEO of five companies and two port districts.

For the 12 years prior to 1971 he served in the U. S. Coast Guard as an pilot of multi-engine amphibians and helicopters.

He is a member of the National Association of Certified Valuators and Analysts (NACVA) and holds the designation Certified Valuation Analyst (CVA) and also the designation Master Analyst in Financial Forensics (MAFF). He also holds the professional designations of CMEA (Certified Machinery & Equipment Appraiser). He is also a member of the International Society of Business Analysts and holds the designation as a CSBA (Certified Senior Business Analyst).

As an appraiser Mr. Barney has performed over 10,000 valuations of business entities, intellectual property and/or equipment. Assignments ranged throughout the full spectrum of industries, from start-ups to billion dollar sales companies.

He holds an M.S. degree in Cybernetic Systems, and a B.A. degree in Management.

He currently President and Managing Partner of American ValueMetrics Corp, an appraisal, consulting, and management services company.

ABOUT AMERICAN VALUEMETRICS

The company is based in Ojai, California, and operates nationally and internationally, specializing in:

- Business Valuations
- Machinery and Equipment Appraisals
- Investment Assessments
- Operational Analyses and Strategic Planning

The author invites any questions or comments on the material covered in this book. He can be reached via the website at:

www.americanvaluemetrics.com